BARBAROSSA
1941

HITLER'S WAR OF ANNIHILATION

BARBAROSSA
1941

HITLER'S WAR OF ANNIHILATION

GEOFFREY MEGARGEE

This edition first published 2007
First published 2006 as *War of Annihilation: Combat and Genocide on the Eastern Front, 1941*.
Published by arrangement with Rowman and Littlefield Publishers, Inc

Tempus Publishing Limited
The Mill, Brimscombe Port,
Stroud, Gloucestershire, GL5 2QG
www.tempus-publishing.com

British Library Cataloguing in Publication Data.
A catalogue record for this book is available from the British Library.

ISBN-13 978 0 7524 4125 2
ISBN-10 0 7524 4125 6

Typesetting and origination by Tempus Publishing Limited

Contents

Abbreviations

AWA	*Allgemeine Wehrmachtamt*, the General Armed Forces Office
BA–MA	Bundesarchiv-Militärarchiv, the federal military archive in Freiburg, Germany
IPN	Instytut Pamieci Narodowej
NARA	National Archives and Records Administration
NIOD	Nederlands Instituut voor Oorlogsdocumentatie
OKH	*Oberkommando des Heeres*, the army high command
OKW	*Oberkommando der Wehrmacht*, the armed forces high command
SD	*Sicherheitsdienst*, the Security Service, the SS intelligence branch
SS	*Schutzstaffel*, a Nazi Party organization that controlled the police and the concentration camps as well as its own military formations. Led by Heinrich Himmler.
USHMM	United States Holocaust Memorial Museum

Preface

The war between Nazi Germany and the Soviet Union was argu-
ably the most important aspect of the Second World War in the
European theater. By far the greatest part of the German army – the
Wehrmacht – served on its eastern front, and most of its losses occurred
there. Without that commitment and those losses, Germany's ultimate
defeat at the hands of the western Allies would have been problematic.
For the USSR, although it emerged victorious, the war was absolutely
devastating. Hundreds of cities and towns lay in ruins at its end, and
somewhere between twenty-five and thirty million Soviet soldiers
and civilians died. The death and destruction resulted not just from
military operations, but because of deliberate policies on the part of
Nazi Germany. The Nazis aimed to kill off a large proportion of the
Soviet population, including all the Jews and Communists they could
lay their hands on. They condemned millions more to death through
starvation, exposure, disease, and forced labor, as part of an aggressive campaign to conquer the east and turn it into a vast colony for
Germany's future benefit. These were policies in which senior members of the German military took an active role, from the planning
phase right through implementation, and in the end their military
misjudgments and inhumanity both contributed to Germany's defeat.

The historical literature on the Nazi-Soviet war has suffered from two fundamental weaknesses, both having to do with the connections between the campaign's military and criminal aspects. The first concerns the German army's reputation. Sometimes, contrary to the popular saying, the losers are the ones who write the history books. This was the case after the Second World War, when former German generals set out to shape the historical image of that conflict. They succeeded to a surprising degree, and that success is nowhere more evident than in the popular understanding of the war in the east. According to their accounts, the Wehrmacht fought a heroic battle against the forces of a barbaric, totalitarian state, and fought honorably, or at least as honorably as it could, given the nature of its enemy. Furthermore, the generals maintained that the blame for the war and for Germany's defeat lay solely with Adolf Hitler, whom they insisted they served only because duty demanded it. Responsibility for any crimes likewise rested with Hitler and his Nazi minions, especially the SS.

The facts are thoroughly at odds with this version of events. Most senior German officers supported the attack against the Soviet Union and believed they would add to the string of easy victories they had won since 1939. They also understood, well before the first soldier set foot across the border, that this was to be a different kind of war than they had fought before. This was to be, quite literally, a *Vernichtungskrieg*, a war of annihilation, in which the army would take an active role in pursuing National Socialism's racist goals. Moreover, when Germany lost the campaign and the war, it would do so not only because of Hitler's inadequacies, but also because its military leadership made fatal mistakes all on its own.

How did the dual myth of German military genius and moral correctness come into being? Several factors contributed. First there was the fundamental difficulty of sorting out such an enormous, complex, and distant series of events. In this case, a unique set of circumstances, having to do with historical sources, compounded the difficulty. When Germany fell, the Allies captured literally millions of pages of reports, speeches, memorandums, private and official diaries, orders, and other records. Not many scholars had access to this material, especially at first, and those who did required decades to make sense of the jumbled mass. In the meantime, the surviving German military leaders brought out their own version of reality in memoirs, letters, interviews, court testimony, and historical studies – some of which the U.S. Army sponsored – in a deliberate effort to shape the historical record of the war. Their material added to the sheer weight of the available material, and it also provided, naturally enough, a clearer, more comprehensive version of events than the raw records could give us, at least at first. Historians were thrilled to have such a resource at their disposal, and many of their works relied heavily on the generals' accounts.

The problem with this situation was that the Germans' stories were flawed in many ways. The men who provided them were not scholars and often did not have access to the original records. Instead they had to rely on their memories, and memories are notoriously unreliable: they rest upon initial perceptions that are subject to a host of biases, and they become increasingly distorted with time. Additionally, the generals had much to hide, especially in connection with their politics and the crimes that their forces had committed, and so they conspired to deceive their audiences on some points. Thus, for reasons both innocent and insidious, their accounts constitute a mix of truth, half-truth, omission, and outright lies that has been difficult to untangle. Professional historians, for their part, skeptical though they were, often did not pick up on the problems in the Germans' accounts. They also had trouble developing a balanced view of events, since Soviet, British, and American records remained unavailable, as did German records that the Soviets captured. And finally, the emerging Cold War shaped the history to a significant degree. With increasing anti-Communist sentiment came a willingness on the part of the public and the military, especially in Germany and America, to accept the generals' version of reality. And despite the end of the Cold War this trend has continued, unfortunately, to the present day, when one-sided accounts by men such as Guderian, von Manstein, and von Mellenthin still find a wide readership.

Since the 1960s, scholars have made great progress in tearing down the myths and disseminating a more accurate depiction of the Nazi-Soviet war. However, the second basic weakness in the literature remained: an artificial division between histories of the military campaigns and accounts of the Nazis' crimes. In part this was an outgrowth of the German generals' efforts, in that they had done their best to pretend that the military operations and the crimes did indeed have no connection with one another. Most military historians, building upon the generals' accounts, have displayed only a passing interest in German occupation policies; they preferred to concentrate instead on the exciting sweep of armies back and forth across the vast spaces of the Soviet Union. Historians who concentrate on the crimes, on the other hand, have often displayed only a superficial understanding of military affairs. As a result, each aspect of the war has appeared to exist more or less in isolation from the other, when in fact they were inextricably linked.

This work aims to bring those two halves together within a brief account of the initial campaign in the east. First I will provide some background on the long-term trends in German thinking and behavior that led up to the conflict. A more detailed narrative will follow, starting with developments after the fall of France in the summer of 1940, when Hitler had to decide what to do next in order to win the war. The account will continue through his decision to attack in the east, cover the military plans that arose from that decision, and describe the battles that followed, up until early 1942, after the Wehrmacht's plans for a single-season victory had failed. Simultaneously, I will describe the Germans' political, economic, and ideological plans for the territories they intended to conquer, the ways in which those plans developed in those first crucial months, and the links between the military and genocidal aspects of the conflict. Only in this way is the course of the eastern war understandable, because of the ways in which the military campaign and the policies of exploitation and murder affected each other's development.

Within the work's larger scheme, I am going to attempt to answer several questions about the German leaders' states of mind. What beliefs, attitudes, and mental habits did they take into the campaign, and how did the military operations develop as a result? More specifically, why did Germany attack the Soviet Union to begin with, and why did its leaders believe they would win? How did their goals and expectations relate to their behavior toward their enemies, on and off the battlefield? How and why did those goals, expectations, and behaviors change as the weeks passed? The answers to these questions will go far toward explaining both the brutality and the ultimate outcome of the Nazi-Soviet war.

I encourage the reader to recognize what this book is not, as well as what it is. It does not present both sides of the story, for one thing; for the most part it offers the German point of view. Although I have added some material on Soviet intentions and actions, for reasons of space I could not go into much detail. That is a frustrating reality, since there are some differences in the two sides' perceptions of the campaign that have yet to be resolved, and also because the work cannot adequately portray the courage and sacrifices of millions of Soviet citizens, without which the Nazis would have won despite their missteps. Second, this is a work of synthesis, not original scholarship; it does not uncover startling new facts so much as put older discoveries together in a new way, and so it depends upon the scholarship of dozens of other historians. At the end you will find a bibliographic essay that discusses many of their works, which you should consult if you want to learn about the eastern campaign, or some aspect of it, in more detail than this book can provide. These limitations notwithstanding, however, I hope that by combining the themes of Wehrmacht military operations and Nazi criminality in one compact work, I will be able to help students and other interested readers to better understand this crucial part of the Second World War.

Acknowledgements

This work could never have come into being without the help of a great many people who contributed in any number of ways. I wish to thank my colleagues in the Center for Advanced Holocaust Studies, including Paul Shapiro, Peter Black, Martin Dean, Patricia Heberer, Wendy Lower, Jürgen Matthäus, Benton Arnovitz, and Severin Hochberg, for their advice and support. Many thanks also to Christopher Browning, Robert Citino, Jürgen Förster, Tim Hogan, Peter Longerich, Randy Papadopoulos, Alex Rossino, Dennis Showalter, Alan Steinweis, Nick Terry, Gerhard Weinberg, and Karl and Sue Wick, who have all given of their time and expertise to help ensure the manuscript's quality and its author's sanity.

Special thanks go to the series editors, Michael A. Barnhart and H. P. Willmott, who conceived of the volume and helped to shape it; to David Glantz, who provided photos from his personal collection as well as many insights into Soviet operations; to Chik and Laurie Shank of Shank Design for their help with the maps; and to the team at Rowman & Littlefield, including Laura Roberts Gottlieb, Andrew Boney, Lynn Weber, Jen Linck, and Jenni Brewer.

The staff members in the National Archives Still Pictures Branch, the Imperial War Museum's Photograph Archive, and the United

States Holocaust Memorial Museum's Library and Photo Archives performed an invaluable service by making those institutions' enormous collections easily accessible.

I would also like to thank my new friend Jury Tyulyubaev for reminding me of the role that the Soviet people played in winning the battle against Nazism. My father, Anthony Scherer Megargee, continues to be a source of inspiration, support, and keen criticism. And, last but certainly not least, my wife Robin has reacted to the long hours, the stress, and the delays to other necessary projects that this work has entailed with boundless patience and encouragement. All of these people helped make this work better. Any remaining deficiencies are my responsibility alone.

The views expressed in this work are the author's and do not necessarily reflect those of the United States Holocaust Memorial Museum.

1

The Roots of the War of Annihilation

To understand what happened in the Soviet Union in the second half of 1941, we could begin our narrative in the latter half of 1940, as concrete planning for the campaign began. To understand *why* it happened, however, we must look farther back, to long-standing cultural and ideological trends, to the First World War and the rise of the Nazi Party, and to developments in the opening months of the Second World War. In doing so we will find that Germany attacked the USSR because of a complicated mix of reasons having to do with ideas on race, nationality, warfare, and domestic and international politics, influences that interacted synergistically to lay the foundations for the events to follow.

Deep Background

Generalizations are dangerous things, and the broader they are, the more flaws there are in them. To attribute a set of attitudes, beliefs, and behaviors to an entire nation is to bring up endless exceptions. To then state that such attitudes, beliefs, and behaviors determined the course of a nation's history is doubly foolhardy, not just because of the initial generalization but because history is a thing of endless contingencies and possibilities. With all that said, however, we may speak of deeply held ideas that shape a nation's destiny, even if they do not determine it.

In Germany's case, particular ideas about race, culture, and nationhood that had been evolving since at least the nineteenth century laid the groundwork for the emergence of Nazism and, too, for the eventual conflict with the Soviet Union, in all its brutality. Put simply, by 1900 many Germans had come to believe in their complete superiority over other peoples, while they also felt that Germany stood under threat from all sides. Foreigners, and especially the Slavs and Jews of central and eastern Europe, became the focus of increasing distrust and hostility. A growing number of Germans believed that conflict with the Slavs was inevitable and that the Jews, too, represented a mortal danger. One should bear in mind that similar beliefs were common among European peoples in this heyday of Western imperialism and racism. Certainly, in their feelings of superiority, the Germans did not outshine the British and French, and the Russians also displayed their own special chauvinism. What, then, explains the fact that these common attitudes took a particularly evil turn in Germany?

To a large extent, the answer lies in the experience of the First World War and its aftermath, which amplified and sharpened some Germans' prejudices. Germany suffered the loss of between 1.8 and 2 million men killed and over 5.5 million wounded in the war, while the home front experienced severe food shortages and civil unrest. The continuing shock to the German system over those four years would be difficult to exaggerate. Many Germans reacted, in part, with increasing calls for conformity and with suspicion of anyone who seemed not to fit in, such as the Jews. Some people suspected the Jews of profiteering and malingering. The army even sponsored a 'Jew count' in 1916, in order to determine what proportion of Jews was serving at the front. (The result, which showed that a *higher* proportion of Jews than non-Jews was serving, did not become public during the conflict.) In the meantime, hundreds of thousands of German soldiers were gaining their first direct experience with the lands to the east, and what they saw often shocked them. The Russian Empire, which included part of the old Polish state, contained a large rural population that was terribly poor by German standards, and the dislocations and disruptions of war made conditions worse. The local population, Jew and gentile alike, seemed alien and primitive to the Germans. Under the combined influence of prejudice and experience, many German soldiers saw the eastern peoples as latently criminal, inferior, dirty, and diseased. From the top command down, many believed that their role was to bring 'civilization' to the region, but that mission gave way in part to feelings of frustration, hopelessness, and disgust as attempts to 'reform' the inhabitants – attempts that were often clumsy, offensive, and even brutal – failed. Many Germans concluded that the easterners were beyond reforming, and that future attempts to control the area would have to take a more absolute form.

The war's end in November 1918 was an additional, terrible blow to the German nation. For four years the army high command had assured the country that it was winning the war. Broad areas of France and most of Belgium were still in German hands, and the Treaty of Brest-Litovsk had taken a huge swath of territory from the defeated Russians, including what is today Poland and Ukraine. The sudden word of the armistice, the abdication of the Kaiser, the creation of a republic, and the accompanying violent political upheavals created an atmosphere of uncertainty that bordered on panic. Later the mood became one of deep anger with the outcome of the war and the injustice (at least in Germans' eyes) that the peace of Versailles forced upon the nation. This was the ground in which the myth of the 'stab in the back' grew. According to this, the German Right's version of reality that the senior army leadership consciously disseminated, the army had not been defeated in the field; instead, Jews and Leftists had taken control of the government and signed a treasonous peace. A new epithet, 'Jewish-Bolshevik,' arose to describe the villains. German Jews found themselves excluded from a wide range of organizations, including veterans' groups and, with rare exceptions, the military. Eastern Jews who attempted to immigrate to Germany, when they got in at all, had to cope with registration and sometimes internment in concentration camps, where the poor conditions led to high rates of illness – thus tending to confirm some people's belief that they were disease carriers to start with. Hostility also took more violent turns as well. Right-wing activists – including some army officers – targeted prominent Jews for assassination, while the so-called Freikorps fought pitched battles with Leftist revolutionaries at home as well as with Poles on the eastern frontier.

One should not exaggerate these trends or make their outcome seem inevitable. Most German Jews, for example, lived comfortable, middle-class lives and enjoyed good relations with their gentile neighbors, even for some time after the National Socialists came to power in 1933. Antisemitism appeared to be much worse in some other countries and was common almost everywhere. The trends were important, however, in that they reflected the attitudes and intentions of those who would eventually make policy in Germany.

The urge to fight 'Jewish Bolshevism' helped form the basis for a natural alliance between the military, which was overwhelmingly conservative, and the Nazi Party, even before the latter took power. The supposed link between Jews and the Left gave the military added incentive to carry out its own antisemitic measures and to support those that the Nazis eventually implemented in civilian society. At the same time, the emergence of the Soviet Union stood out as an additional threat to the east. Some officers favored friendly relations with the USSR, and there was even some secret military cooperation during the 1920s. Over time, however, the dominant line of thought in military circles came to correspond with Hitler's. He believed that a German aristocracy had governed Russia before 1917, but that the Bolshevik Revolution had put the Jews in power over the mass of Slavs, who were, by his definition, incapable of ruling themselves. And since Bolshevism was, by its nature, an avowedly expansionist ideology, most German officers came to the conclusion that the USSR was a danger to Germany and to Western civilization more generally. In their Weltanschauung, or world view, antisemitic, anti-Slav, and anti-Marxist elements thus combined in a new way to support expansion to the east, which had long been a goal of the German Right in any case.

Expansion was also, of course, one of Nazism's central goals. By the early 1920s, Hitler had combined his hatred of the Jews and of the supposedly Jewish-dominated Soviet state with existing calls to conquer additional Lebensraum, or living space, in the east. He tied this idea in with Romantic notions having to do with blood and soil, and with German eastward migration going back as much as six centuries, but his strongest reasons were more immediate. In his view, Germany needed more land in order to support a growing population and take up a position as a world power. 'The right to possess soil can become a duty if without extension of its soil a great nation seems doomed to destruction,' he wrote in *Mein Kampf*. 'And most especially when not some little nigger nation or other is involved, but the Germanic mother of life, which has given the present-day world its cultural picture.' Such expansion could have only one target: 'If we speak of soil in Europe today, we can primarily have in mind only Russia and her vassal border states.'[1]

That the quest for Lebensraum would require aggressive war was a fact that the military accepted as a matter of course, for a variety of reasons. First, a growing number of right-wing Germans believed in a loose ideology that we now know as Social Darwinism, which applies elements of Charles Darwin's evolutionary theory of biology to human societies. According to this belief system, conflict is inevitable, between individuals and nations as between animal species, and only the strong deserve to survive. This was a fundamental principle of Nazism. Hitler wrote in his second (unpublished) book that politics must always be 'the struggle of a nation for its existence' in which such ideas as an alternative between peace and war 'immediately sink into nothingness.'[2] So, too, did concerns over the rights of other peoples disappear: since Germans were clearly superior, they deserved to take what they needed, by force if necessary, no matter what the consequences for their opponents.

In the aftermath of the Great War, the brutality inherent in this approach became a dominant theme in itself, a broad social movement of which the Nazis took advantage. In a concrete sense, the war had brought previously unimagined violence and destruction into people's lives. The effects were profound. For the Right, especially, war became a model for life, and Germans in general became more used to brutality, regardless of the target. Political discussion in the postwar era took on aggressive, militaristic overtones, and actual political violence reached new heights. A group of thinkers with the paradoxical name 'conservative revolutionaries,' who drew their inspiration from a mythical brotherhood of the trenches, promoted war as a positive good, a force that would eliminate society's weaklings and create a 'New Man' who would embody self-discipline, ruthlessness, courage, and nationalism. They promised a new, more egalitarian society, cultural rejuvenation, and an end to the corruption and privilege of the old regime. The Nazis used these themes, which they reinforced with their own political violence, to establish a strong political base that the military admired and coveted. And when the next war came, the politics of brutality would influence military operations and occupation policy.

Such cultural undercurrents, in combination with conservative racial and political beliefs, found more concrete expression in the military's vision of the coming war. First and foremost, for Germany's senior military leaders, war was virtually the only, and certainly the final, arbiter of international affairs. Moreover, they believed that war was inevitable if Germany hoped to ensure its future, first as a state, then as a European power, and, ultimately, as a world power. In fact, in their eyes (as in those of other German conservatives) the Great War had never really ended. Germany still faced powerful enemies, both within and without, whose destruction they believed to be essential. In May 1925 a Defense Ministry document stated, 'That Germany will in the future have to fight a war for its continued existence as a people and state is certain.'³ For that reason Hitler's generals shared his goal of rearming Germany, materially and psychologically, and then putting that military strength to use. The new chancellor made that intention clear to his senior military leaders only three days after he assumed power; at a dinner on 3 February 1933, he told the assembled officers that he planned, among other things, to rebuild a standing army, to regain a position of power for Germany, and to use that power, in all likelihood, to expand to the east. That was exactly what his audience wanted to hear.

In thinking about a future war, the senior officers' intellectual starting point was the concept of 'total war,' a vague but broadly accepted set of assumptions about the nature of the conflict to come, according to which all of society's resources would have to be channeled toward one goal: military victory. Those assumptions had begun to evolve even before the Great War, but that conflict strengthened them by calling upon German society to an unprecedented degree. According to postwar military thinking, however, Germany had never achieved its potential, and the failure to mobilize society completely had paved the way for the 'stab in the back.' There could be no such failure next time. The military looked to the regime to reshape society in every aspect: political, ideological, economic, and military. No source of weakness or disunity – such as pluralism, pacifism, or racial mixing – was tolerable. Propaganda would hammer home the absolute nature of the struggle and highlight every perceived grievance and supposed threat. Economic preparations would have to meet the needs of both the military and the home front, so that the nation would have the physical and psychological stamina it would need for a long fight. In broad terms, the military approved of the Nazis' attempts to create something called a *Volksgemeinschaft*, a racial community, in which homogeneity of blood and thought would provide the strength and support for an aggressive, expansionist, and protracted war – or, put another way, a *Wehrgemeinschaft*, a community of arms, a completely militarized society. The task of forming that society was one that the generals wanted to leave to the civilian government, and the Nazis, for their part, were ready to provide just such assistance: hence their appeal to officers who otherwise viewed some of the more radical aspects of Nazism with suspicion. Hitler's defense minister, General Werner von Blomberg, said to a group of his fellow generals that Nazism represented 'a broad national desire and the realization of that toward which many of the best have been striving for years.'[4]

The 'total war' idea was also significant for strategy (the realm of warfare that involves the timing, targets, and purposes of war) as well as for operations (the conduct of military campaigns) and for occupation policy. Since it encompassed not just the activities of the fighting forces but the material and moral foundations of the nation's war effort, in offensive terms 'total war' targeted every source of enemy strength for destruction or exploitation. There would be no distinction between soldiers and civilians in any future war, since the latter supported the former. In a battle for the survival of the race and the nation, any measure that would break the enemy's will, deprive him of the means to fight, or add to Germany's fighting power at his expense was, by definition, not only allowable but essential.

Here the connections between the 'total war' idea and some long-evolving trends in German military theory and practice came to the fore. At least since the Franco-Prussian War (1870–1871), Germans had been developing an approach to warfare that emphasized the maximum application of violence. On the battlefield this meant the 'battle of annihilation,' in which the goal was not just to drive the enemy from the field but to destroy them as a fighting force. Behind the lines in conquered territory it meant extraordinarily harsh repressive measures that aimed to crush any resistance on the part of the civilian population. The military might still observe the rules of warfare, but as a matter of convenience, not of principle. Even before 1914, German legal and military thinkers were denying the legitimacy of international laws of war. They believed that 'military necessity' would always overrule any limitations on violence. The scale of German crimes in the First World War would never come close to that in the Second, but the Germans did execute prisoners of war and civilian hostages, pillage and burn towns, and even use groups of civilians as human shields, all of which practices violated international agreements that Germany had signed. And little changed after the war; for example, in a draft regulation on the supply of the army, dated 1 April 1935, then-Major Eduard Wagner, who later would oversee all army supply and rear-area security operations, wrote that the army's first task was to secure enemy territory for its own supply and to enlist the native population in forced labor.

The Germans' approach to warfare would combine with racism and political ideology to make the coming war extraordinarily brutal, especially in the east. Hitler made his intentions clear in the first meeting with his senior generals: the best use of Germany's reestablished political power would be 'the conquest of new living space in the east and its ruthless Germanization.'[5] For Hitler and the Nazis, this was an ideological constant, not a political expedient. Before another gathering of officers on 10 February 1939, he reemphasized that Germany's present Lebensraum was too small; the only solution was to take more. And he left no doubt as to the nature of the coming conflict: 'a purely ideological war, i.e. consciously a national and racial war.' On 23 November of that same year, he again told his commanders, 'A racial struggle has erupted about who is to dominate in Europe and the world.'[6] Certainly his audience could have been in no doubt as to his seriousness by that time, since the Wehrmacht (meaning all the armed forces, but also used to refer to the army) and the SS and police had been acting with unprecedented viciousness in occupied Poland for nearly three months. In any event, there is little indication that any of the officers disagreed with their Führer, and none that they did so effectively.

Beyond the values and goals that the generals shared with Hitler, there were other, even more deeply rooted reasons for this kind of acquiescence. These had to do with fundamental ideas on leadership and responsibility. The subject is complex, but it helps to explain why those German officers who did not share the most radical parts of Hitler's Weltanschauung were nonetheless willing to carry out his orders. It also helps us to understand how those officers who supported the regime and participated in its crimes attempted to justify their actions later on, to themselves and to posterity.

Earlier in its history, the German (earlier Prussian) officer corps had demonstrated a capacity for intellectual and moral independence, even at the political level. In 1812, General Hans von Yorck had defected, with his army, from Napoleon's service, thus forcing Prussia to fight against the French. And in 1918, contrary to the myth, the Supreme Army Command was the agency that forced the German government to sue for peace. Thus German officers had demonstrated that, when they considered the issue to be important enough, they would stand up to even the highest authority. Within a narrower military sphere, moreover, the General Staff, that elite body of German officers that came to dominate the command system, especially during and after the Great War, had long recognized the need for a kind of disciplined, institutionalized independence of thought. In the German army, unlike others, a chief of staff – that is, a commander's principal adviser – shared responsibility with his commander for any order, and could appeal an order with which he disagreed; this was known as the principle of joint responsibility. Additionally, and again in contrast with the practice in other armies, a lower-ranking German officer could exercise authority over others of higher rank, when circumstances dictated. That being said, German officers also valued obedience and loyalty, as do officers in most armies; they did not lightly question their orders or assume authority to which they were not entitled.

Plainly, though, the officer corps demonstrated little independence in its relationship with Hitler. After the war, officers made much of the personal oath of loyalty that they swore to their Führer; it did not differ substantially from that which officers had sworn to kings and emperors in times past, and on its face it called for unconditional obedience. It also meshed perfectly with one of the central principles of Nazism: the *Führerprinzip*, or 'leader principle,' according to which all authority and responsibility flowed from the top downward and the subordinate's only duty was to carry out his orders to the letter, without question. If we believe their memoirs, the generals chafed under this system but were powerless to do anything about it because of the oath they had sworn and their duty as military men. They also tried to portray themselves as apolitical servants of the regime who had restricted their activities to strictly military matters.

Two sets of facts weaken those arguments, however. The first concerns the Prussian officer corps's tradition of independence at the political level, as we noted earlier. In addition, one must also account for the officer corps's behavior in the years between the end of the First World War and the beginning of Hitler's rule. In that period, officers swore a number of oaths. First and foremost, they swore an oath to uphold the constitution and the legal institutions of the Weimar Republic. As part and parcel of that oath, they were also obliged to follow the terms of any international agreements to which their government was a party. Those included the Versailles treaty, which restricted the size and structure of the German military, and the Locarno pacts, by which Germany essentially pledged not to go to war against its western neighbors. These were all obligations that senior German officers routinely, casually, and even enthusiastically violated in pursuit of both professional and political goals. From that fact one can gather that an oath, in and of itself, held no particular power for them.

A more complete explanation for the officers' obedience must include other elements as well. Certainly the goals, interests, and attitudes that the generals shared with their Führer formed a solid foundation for their loyalty, first of all. On a less concrete but still important level, shared leadership philosophies were also a factor. True, at face value the traditions of the General Staff were in conflict with the *Führerprinzip*, but that conflict was actually not as important as some officers made it seem later on. For one thing, the General Staff officially abandoned the principle of joint responsibility as early as 1939; the basic staff regulation recognized that the commander, not his adviser, bore ultimate responsibility and authority. If this was not a call for blind obedience, it was at least an acknowledgment that the relationship between commanders and staff officers had changed. At the same time, a more careful examination of the *Führerprinzip* reveals a system that was not really so rigid as it appeared on the surface. It depended not so much on a vision that the commander imposed on his subordinates, but more on a common set of goals and assumptions that they all shared. In political terms, as Hitler put it, 'The Führer is the Party and the Party is the Führer.'[7] Or, on another occasion: 'The commander must give orders that express the common feelings of his men.'[8] The *Führerprinzip* did not eliminate initiative, but rather emphasized a common purpose and shared responsibility. There are parallels here, too, to the General Staff's system for selecting and training its personnel, which had for decades ensured nearly homogeneous political views and also attempted to instill a common way of thinking that combined accepted principles with initiative and flexibility. And there are connections with the army's efforts, after the Great War, to break down the social barriers that had separated officers and men, as well as to later steps that made officers responsible for political indoctrination. All of this adds up to a command system that provided for both obedience and initiative in pursuit of a common aim, with a high degree of teamwork.

The Germans' understanding of leadership and responsibility gave soldiers and civilians alike a convenient degree of moral as well as practical flexibility. Those who agreed with their orders could carry them out with initiative and imagination. An oath, in and of itself, meant little; the oath to Hitler was different precisely because most officers believed in the individual, and hence in the system, to which they were swearing allegiance. The oath could also provide a cover, as well: those who had qualms about their orders could tell themselves – and others – that they were just following orders, and that 'political matters' were none of their affair anyway. Members of the army used such reasoning quite unselfconsciously. For example, in July 1938, when the chief of the General Staff, General Ludwig Beck, was worried about Hitler's expressed desire to attack Czechoslovakia, one of Beck's former subordinates, Colonel Erich von Manstein, wrote to Beck that if Hitler wanted to issue the order, then he, not the army, would have to accept the responsibility. To von Manstein, Beck's belief that the resulting war would ruin Germany was secondary. Similar rationalizations appeared after the war, when German officers had to confront both Germany's defeat and the criminal nature of the war they had unleashed.

This, then, was the constellation of beliefs, attitudes, and assumptions that contributed to the German leadership's willingness to fight a war of conquest and genocide: faith in their own superiority; loathing of Jews and Slavs; fear and hatred of Marxism and conflation of it with Jewishness; belief in existential struggle and in Germany's right to use any means to win; attachment to ideals of brutality and ruthlessness; a desire for another war and the assumption that such a war would be 'total'; particular hostility toward the Soviet Union; and principles of leadership and responsibility that would, in effect, act to facilitate criminal behavior. The last ingredient would be the war itself, in which all these factors would work together to produce effects that even the most cynical generals had not foreseen.

Dress Rehearsal: Poland

Until relatively recently, most historians who examined the German military's crimes during the Second World War tended not to focus on the Polish campaign of 1939, but rather to skip ahead to 1941 and the invasion of the Soviet Union. The German invasion of Poland has long had a reputation as a 'clean' campaign, in which the army fought honorably. Although the five years of German occupation were perhaps the cruelest in Poland's long history, the SS and Nazi civilian administrators received the blame, while the Wehrmacht maintained a positive image. Newer historical works have established, however, that in reality the German army worked with the SS in Poland in much the same way that they would cooperate later in the USSR, even though the war against the Soviet Union was a more openly ideological conflict from the start. Therefore we need to look at the Polish campaign in some detail if we are to understand the evolutionary process that led up to the war of annihilation later on.

German attitudes toward Poland and the Poles reflected the broader biases against Slavs and Jews that we examined earlier, as well as frustrations and resentments that came out of the First World War and the Versailles treaty. German hostility toward Poles went back at least to the eighteenth century. Poland as a country had ceased to exist after Prussia, Russia, and Austria partitioned it in three successive stages in 1772, 1793, and 1795. For the next century and more, the Germans attempted to 'civilize' their parts of Poland by importing German settlers, political forms, and culture. The Poles had, understandably, resented and resisted these measures, much to the chagrin of the Germans; the most important net effect had been to increase hostility on both sides. Then, with German defeat in 1918, the Poles had risen up to throw off German rule. Fierce local fighting between Polish and German paramilitary units, with accompanying atrocities, had continued even after the Allies dictated the re-creation of a Polish state as part of the peace settlement; only in 1923 did it finally die down, but tension remained high on both sides of the new border. Germans believed that they had been deprived of territory that rightly belonged to them, while the Poles maintained that they were only getting their own back. The Polish minority in eastern Germany and the German minority in western Poland were both the targets of widespread distrust, and some persecution, by the respective governing majorities. Throughout the Weimar and Nazi years, German hostility toward Poles and Polish Jews increased dramatically. Political pressure groups kept up a steady drumbeat in favor of reconquest in the east. Newspaper stories, magazine articles, public lectures, and even schoolbooks repeated the messages that Poles were treacherous, stupid, and barbaric, that Polish territory rightfully belonged to Germany, and that Jews (over three million of whom lived in Poland) were Germany's mortal enemies. Hitler signed a nonaggression pact with Poland in 1934, but this was an expedient measure that did little to change attitudes in either country. Given this background, neither the fact of the invasion of Poland nor its nature is terribly surprising.

Concrete planning for the invasion began in the spring of 1939. By that time Hitler had decided on the path he would take to his long-term goal of acquiring Lebensraum in the USSR and simultaneously destroying the Jewish-Bolshevik state there. He had already chalked up an impressive string of bloodless foreign policy victories, starting with the remilitarization of the Rhineland in 1936 and culminating, most recently, with the occupation of the Czech provinces of Bohemia and Moravia in March 1939. That latest move, however, was the last that he would accomplish without war. The British and French, having forced the Czechoslovak government to hand over a sizeable slice of territory to Germany the previous autumn in exchange for peace, now recognized that Hitler wanted more than a few minor border adjustments, and they were determined not to allow him to expand any further. Hitler, for his part, noted that war with France and Britain was inevitable, and would have to come before he began his major push for Lebensraum in the east, lest Germany again find itself in a two-front war. Similarly, in order to strike at them, he needed to make sure that his eastern flank would be secure. With Czechoslovakia out of the picture, Poland was the only bordering state that posed a threat. Hitler pressured Warsaw to join the German sphere, but the Polish government recognized that this would mean their complete subordination to Germany and refused to acquiesce; they might go down fighting, but they would not surrender the independence their nation had dreamt of for over a century. On 25 March Hitler instructed the commander in chief of the army, General Walther von Brauchitsch, to begin planning for the invasion.

Up to this time, Poland had not really figured in Hitler's larger goals, in spite of the hostility that he and most other Germans shared toward their eastern neighbor. His focus remained on the Soviet Union throughout the years up to 1939; to the extent that he thought about Poland at all, he tended to think of it as a bulwark against Bolshevism, or even a possible junior partner that he could pressure into making territorial concessions and helping to destroy the Soviets, with whom the Poles had already fought a war in 1920–1921. In the spring of 1939, however, this state of affairs changed. Now Hitler began to think of Poland as one more source of Lebensraum and to give free rein to his hostility and racism. He and the head of the SS, *Reichsführer* Heinrich Himmler, agreed on large territorial annexations: Poles and Jews would be pushed out of those areas so that Germans could settle there. In May Hitler stated to his senior military leaders that he intended to exploit Poland fully and use Poles as a labor force for Germans. For the moment he did not elaborate, but the planning processes within the military and the Nazi Party were already intersecting to lay the groundwork for a brutal campaign.

The plan for the actual military operations evolved smoothly over the spring and summer. General Franz Halder, the chief of the Army General Staff in the OKH (*Oberkommando des Heeres*, or Army High Command), was enthusiastic about the attack. He commented to a gathering of army officers that with the end of the artificial friendliness between the two states, 'a stone has fallen from our hearts.'[9] He went on to predict an easy victory in two or three weeks, even if Britain and France intervened. Near the end of April General von Brauchitsch presented the army's draft plan to Hitler, who approved it without significant changes.

In addition to the main plan of operations, the army also had to deal with the issue of rear area security and administration. Because the plan of attack called for rapid advances on narrow fronts, many Polish troops and armed civilians were certain to wind up behind the German front lines. These forces, if unchecked, could create problems for the German supply and administration troops that followed along behind the front. If severe enough, those problems could even affect the pace of the advance by interrupting the flow of supplies and forcing the diversion of combat forces to police the rear area. The Germans' approach to solving this problem, to which the idea of total war lent a kind of intellectual justification, was to counter any resistance with the utmost brutality, in the belief that they could cow the population into passivity and even, perhaps, collaboration. In line with that approach, on 24 July 1939, General Wagner, now the army's quartermaster general, issued a set of special regulations that authorized German troops to take and execute hostages in the event of attacks by snipers or irregulars. In some regions German forces were also to detain all Polish males – Jewish and gentile – between the ages of seventeen and forty-five as prisoners of war, whether found armed or not. And because front-line combat troops were in high demand, the army's leaders quickly decided to use SS and police units to augment their own forces for security tasks. Halder informed his subordinates on the general staff of such plans as early as April, and the SS began putting together its preparations in early May.

By the spring of 1939 the SS – for *Schutzstaffel*, or 'protective echelon,' originally Hitler's personal bodyguard – was becoming an increasingly powerful institution within the Nazi Party, and it would draw forces from several different subordinate organizations in order to carry out its tasks in Poland. It controlled all the police forces in Germany: the uniformed *Ordnungspolizei* (Order Police, also known as the Orpo) and the plainclothes *Sicherheitspolizei* (Security Police, or Sipo). The Sipo, in turn, included the ordinary detectives of the *Kriminalpolizei* (Criminal Police, or Kripo) and the *Geheime Staatspolizei* (Secret State Police, or Gestapo), which handled political offenses. The SS also had its own intelligence branch, the *Sicherheitsdienst* (Security Service, or SD), which existed parallel to the Sipo. And the SS could draw upon its own military force, which was still small at this stage but deeply imbued with Nazi ideology. In early July, Reinhard Heydrich, the head of the Security Police and SD, ordered the formation of four *Einsatzgruppen*, or task groups, each to consist of approximately five hundred men from the Sipo, the Kripo, the Gestapo, and the SD; reinforcements would bring the total number of *Einsatzgruppen* personnel to over four thousand before the campaign began. These, along with other kinds of SS detachments, would be the Nazis' strike forces in Poland. They would gather up the records of groups that the Germans deemed dangerous, such as anti-German underground organizations, Jews, Freemasons, and members of the Catholic Church hierarchy and Leftist parties. They would secure Polish police records and deal with 'normal' criminals. They would establish networks of informants and collaborators. And they would deal with political and racial opponents, including those taken in action against German troops and those whose names appeared on special lists of wanted individuals.

From the start, the SS and the army coordinated their plans for the activities of the *Einsatzgruppen*. At the end of July, Wagner met with Heydrich to solidify those plans. The resulting SS guidelines stated, 'By agreement with the Army High Command . . . the task of the Security Police *Einsatzkommandos* [subunits of the *Einsatzgruppen*] is combating all elements in foreign territory and behind the fighting troops that are hostile to the Reich and German people. [10] Later orders enjoined the *Einsatzgruppen* commanders to maintain close contact with all local military commanders, the chiefs of civil administration, and the Order Police. For its part, the army made sure to integrate the *Einsatzgruppen* into its military security operations. Army intelligence and quartermaster officers would coordinate with the *Einsatzgruppen* and could deploy them as needed within their geographic areas of responsibility. They would also control normal military police – the *Feldgendarmarie* – as well as the *Geheime Feldpolizei*, the Secret Field Police, which was responsible for counterespionage, gathering intelligence on resistance movements, and surveillance of German troops. Other military units and the Order Police would also operate in the rear areas; close coordination was necessary to ensure that such operations went smoothly. As for the targets of all this activity, the Security Police was busy gathering information for the wanted persons lists, with assistance from the military's counterintelligence office, known as the *Abwehr*. The *Abwehr* drew up its own lists of people to be arrested, foremost among whom were suspected saboteurs and espionage agents, and forwarded those lists to the SS.

The working relationship between the army and the SS contained the seeds of conflict, however, because the army was not privy to all the SS plans. The army wanted to arrest Poles who might resist German domination and certainly would not have hesitated to carry out executions on a large scale in reaction to such resistance. The SS, on the other hand, was planning to shoot large numbers of civilians as a preemptive measure, in order to deprive Poland of its political, spiritual, and intellectual leadership. Heydrich would later state that Hitler gave him a personal order to kill thousands of Polish leaders; the name for this operation was *Tannenberg*. On 18 August Heydrich briefed the *Einsatzgruppen* commanders and their principal subordinates on the mission. He lectured them on atrocities that Poles were allegedly committing against ethnic Germans in Poland. He informed them that their units would have to maintain order in the army's rear, and that they could expect certain underground resistance organizations to put up stiff resistance. And he pointed out that Poland's intelligentsia formed the core of such resistance – without, however, coming right out and saying that they were to be shot. Instead he referred to the measures that the *Einsatzgruppen* could take, which included arrests and shootings. Moreover, in the same meeting the *Einsatzgruppen* commanders received copies of the wanted persons lists, which by then contained the names of 61,000 Poles, including clergymen, political leaders, and Communists.

At this point the invasion was less than two weeks away, and now Hitler revealed more of his intentions to his military leaders. On 22 August 1939, he called them together at his retreat at Berchtesgaden, where he held forth at length on the situation with Poland. According to anonymous notes from the conference, he revealed to them that he was close to concluding a nonaggression pact with the Soviet Union, which would remove the single most important obstacle to an invasion. He also stated that, for him, 'the goal of the war [lies] not in reaching a certain line, but in the physical destruction of the enemy.'[11] He went on to say that he had SS units standing by to kill Polish men, women, and children; that only in that way would Germany win the Lebensraum it needed; that Poland would be depopulated and settled by Germans. Unfortunately we do not have any record of the officers' reactions to these pronouncements. Perhaps at least some of them thought that Hitler was exaggerating and that since they would control the theater of war, they could prevent any excesses. If so, they were mistaken.

The military campaign against Poland opened on 1 September 1939, and was never really in doubt. The Poles, for patriotic, geographic, and economic reasons, spread their forces out in an effort to hold the entire length of their border, which presented the Germans with no natural obstacles. The Poles also lacked modern equipment, and they mobilized late. Their task was hopeless. The Germans punched through the defenses with relative ease and raced for the interior of the country, while the Luftwaffe cleared the skies of Polish planes and decimated Polish troops on the ground. The declaration of war by the British and French on 3 September caused the Germans some concern but had little practical effect. On 17 September the Soviets, in accordance with a secret clause in their nonaggression pact with Germany, moved into eastern Poland, but this move merely accelerated the inevitable. By the time the Soviets entered the conflict, the Wehrmacht had been on the outskirts of Warsaw for days. The defenders there held out bravely, even after the Germans began an aerial and artillery bombardment of the city, but they could only do so much. At the end of the month the city surrendered, and organized resistance in Poland came to an end. The Germans had lost 11,000 killed, 30,000 wounded, and 3,400 missing; the Poles lost 70,000 killed, 133,000 wounded, and 700,000 prisoners, not including their losses while fighting the Soviets. By the standards of the last war, this had been an incredibly rapid and cheap victory for the Wehrmacht.

With that said, the campaign was also a particularly brutal one. The Poles, for their part, did forcibly remove ethnic German civilians from the border areas to counter the very real threat from German paramilitary units. In fact, some clashes took place between ethnic Germans and the Polish army, and thousands of ethnic Germans suffered abuse and sometimes death at the hands of the Poles. At the same time, Polish paramilitary units, whose members numbered in the tens of thousands, resisted the German invasion in any way they could – such as by sniping at German soldiers. Such incidents fueled the German troops' hostility, which the Nazi regime and their commanders had done their best to reinforce in any case. Stories of supposed Polish iniquity and the evils of the Versailles treaty had been standard fare for some time. So, too, had been injunctions to show no leniency toward the enemies of the Reich. Long-standing prejudices, propaganda, official sanction, and the stress of war all came together to produce swift, merciless repressive measures. Civilians found with weapons – even antiques, in some cases – were often shot out of hand; so were so-called plunderers. Poles whom ethnic Germans implicated in atrocities were also summarily executed. Hostages were arrested and shot en masse in retaliation for partisan attacks; often they were community leaders, women, and children, and in some cases the orders for such retributive measures came from Hitler personally. German troops sometimes executed Polish soldiers and civilian irregulars alike after they surrendered, and destroyed whole apartment blocks after snipers opened fire from them. In some areas the Wehrmacht and the *Einsatzgruppen* rounded up all adult males; German authorities interrogated them, and those whose names appeared on the wanted persons lists were either shot or deported to concentration camps in Germany. By the end of the campaign in early October the Wehrmacht alone had executed at least 16,000 Poles, and perhaps as many as 27,000, as a result of proceedings that it looked upon as official and proper. Thousands more died as a result of spontaneous shootings and mass executions by the *Einsatzgruppen*. In most of these actions there was close cooperation between the SS, the army, and the police.

Operations against Polish Jews also began almost as soon as the campaign opened. In the southern Polish region of East Upper Silesia, for example, which the Germans intended to annex, the Special Purpose *Einsatzgruppe* von Woyrsch, named for its commander, Udo von Woyrsch, entered Polish territory on 6 September and immediately began a reign of terror, with the goal of inducing Jews to flee eastward out of the region and into the future Soviet zone. The group attacked Jewish shops, destroyed synagogues, and beat and murdered hundreds of Jewish men, women, and children. The orders for this policy came directly from the top of the SS hierarchy. Apparently Hitler, Himmler, and Heydrich had, at this stage of the war, decided to establish a Jewish 'reservation' to the east (there was as yet no plan to exterminate them). The army often cooperated in such measures, in part by securing the line of demarcation with the Soviet zone and preventing any Jews, as well as Poles, from crossing westward into the area under German control. On some occasions army units also carried out expulsions on their own authority. In this way over 20,000 Jews were forced out of the region. Much the same pattern held in northern Poland, as well.

This is not to say that relations between the army and the SS were always smooth. In some instances the army resisted SS attempts to round up and shoot unarmed civilians out of hand, out of the context of any overtly hostile act against German forces, and at times army officers even tried to prevent the summary execution of known members of Polish underground groups. Army officers also sometimes objected to the vicious attacks on Jews and to the widespread SS looting of valuables from Jewish homes and businesses. The army and the SS sometimes came into open conflict, with the local army commander appealing up the chain of command to one of the army group commanders, and the local SS officer citing orders that Himmler or even Hitler himself had issued. Army commanders in Poland even insisted upon the arrest and court martial of some SS personnel, although Hitler would reverse their convictions in a blanket amnesty on 4. October And the divisions went all the way to the top. Wagner went to Heydrich on 19 September to protest SS behavior, and von Brauchitsch did the same with Hitler on 20 September. In both cases the army officers received assurances that the measures had been planned but that the SS would strive to minimize army involvement in the future. Those assurances apparently satisfied the officers; von Brauchitsch sent out an order to his senior commanders the next day, in which he explained that Hitler had assigned the *Einsatzgruppen* certain 'ethnic-political tasks' that were outside the army's responsibility.[12] He stipulated that military police units were not to become involved in such tasks, and otherwise told his commanders not to interfere.

Von Brauchitsch's order highlights the mindset of those officers at the top and middle levels of the hierarchy. They were worried less about the rights and welfare of Polish citizens than about the officer corps's authority and the discipline of their troops. *Ordnung* – order – was foremost in the commanders' minds. They expected SS units operating in their areas to obey their instructions. They also did not want their troops running amok, shooting and looting in civilian areas; such a breakdown in discipline could affect combat performance. For form's sake they preferred to see suspects tried, even if such trials offered little in the way of justice: military judges sentenced an average of two hundred Poles to death every day. But if Hitler authorized the SS to take 'radical measures,' so be it. The generals simply preferred that such measures be kept out of sight. In other words, as long as they could strictly control the circumstances under which army units participated in actions against Polish and Polish-Jewish civilians, the army's leaders were not inclined to protest. At the lower levels there were soldiers who found SS brutality repulsive, but they appear to have been in the minority, and their senior commanders, meanwhile, continued to support the policy, just so long as they did not have to get their hands too dirty.

Poland thus provides a link, an intermediate stage that connects the long-term trends in German political and military policy toward the peoples of the east with the overtly ideological war of annihilation that would follow in the Soviet Union less than two years later. Germans had long had a problematic relationship with Slavs, and most Germans viewed the Polish state as a criminal abomination. The millions of Jews there served as an additional target. The dominant German view toward war, which incorporated belief in its utility with an emphasis on maximum brutality, lent itself to a war with Poland, as it would later with the Soviet Union. The military had long seen the application of brutality as the best way to deal with civilian resistance, and they applied it consistently in the 1939 campaign. The SS carried that campaign a step farther than many in the army were ready to go, but the generals worked out an acceptable compromise without undue effort, and in the future both sides would make sure that such friction as arose would not occur again. The next time, the invading army would be fully informed and prepared for the *Volkstumskampf*, the battle of races, that Hitler and his immediate subordinates – Nazi Party and military – intended to carry out.

2

Plans and Preparations, 1940–1941

The close connection between the military campaign in the Soviet Union and the crimes that the army and the SS committed there did not develop unexpectedly after operations began. Rather, it was the culmination of a planning process that went on for nearly a year before a single German soldier set foot in the USSR. Almost from the moment that process began, the principals understood that the coming war would be unlike any conflict in modern history, both in terms of its scale and because of the ideologically driven policies that would shape it.

The Decision to Attack

On 22 June 1940, the French signed an armistice with Germany, after the Wehrmacht drove the British off the Continent and destroyed the French army in a matter of seven weeks. Hitler then embarked on a tour of Paris and the battlefields where he had fought in the First World War. He saw no reason to deny himself a break; after all, he reasoned, the war in the west was over. Like most Germans, he believed the British would quickly see the hopelessness of their position and sue for peace. The German army was the best in the world; Germany now controlled the territory and resources of Poland, Czechoslovakia, the Netherlands, Belgium, Norway, Denmark, Luxembourg, and France; and the Soviet Union, the one power that could pose an immediate threat, was bending over backward to stay on good terms. Surely the British would be accommodating, since they lacked the means for any effective action.

The British, however, proved intransigent. From Prime Minister Winston Churchill on down, they demonstrated that they had no intention of surrendering. This left Hitler facing a strategic dilemma. France's sudden collapse had been a shock, albeit a pleasant one, and no one had prepared for a next step, either physically or psychologically. How could Germany now bring the war to a successful conclusion? In the coming months Hitler and his military commanders would struggle with the problem. The Führer's most senior military planner, General Alfred Jodl, produced an initial assessment of Germany's options on 30 June. In it he suggested, as one possibility, air and naval attacks on the Royal Air Force (RAF), manufacturing centers, supplies, and shipping, as well as terror attacks on population centers (which he justified as 'retribution' – for what, he did not make clear). He also called for immediate preparations for an invasion, should the British still refuse to come to terms. As an alternative (or perhaps in combination; here again he was not clear), Jodl suggested strikes against the British Empire, possibly with the help of other European states.

Thus began a period of strategic confusion for the Germans. None of the courses of action in Jodl's memo would produce a quick victory, and Hitler knew that. He also had neither the background nor the temperament to deal with this kind of problem. He had served with some distinction as an enlisted man in the First World War, but that experience in no way prepared him for supreme command. By nature he tended to be impulsive, intuitive, and stubborn. He possessed a certain raw talent for strategy – often more than his generals – but he frequently based his assessments of other nations on inadequate information and the most simplistic biases. He did have long-range goals that were never far from his thoughts: the destruction of the 'Jewish-Bolshevik' state to the east and the acquisition of Lebensraum there. In deciding on the means to those ends he was an opportunist, however, and the present situation offered no clear opportunities. He knew he could not leave the British unmolested forever – their economic power, and the blockade they had imposed on the Continent, would start to tell with time – but he could see no way to defeat them. His military advisers were also out of their depth. Despite long careers in the military, they were mentally ill-equipped to make broad strategic judgments; they could offer no good suggestions. And so, typically, Hitler chose at first not to choose. Instead he tried to pursue several options at the same time, in the vague hope that one of them would yield the result he wanted.

Direct attacks against the British Isles seemed to offer the best prospect of a quick decision. Hitler rejected terror bombing at first, because he still hoped for a deal with the British government. He also rejected unlimited submarine warfare, because he was not yet ready for the conflict that such operations might spark with the United States. His preferred method was to mount air attacks against the RAF, gain air superiority to counter the Royal Navy's advantage in ships, and then launch a seaborne invasion. He issued the first order to this effect on 2 July and watched the progress of planning and operations carefully thereafter. Soon German planes were attacking coastal targets, then the RAF air bases, and finally, as the summer passed and the British continued fighting, civilian areas. By the middle of September, however, the Luftwaffe had clearly lost the battle, and with the army and navy bickering over the invasion plans, Hitler eventually postponed the attack until the following spring. In truth, few of his planners took the prospect seriously any longer.

While preparations for the invasion went forward that summer, Hitler also considered ways to strike at key points in the British Empire, especially Gibraltar: by sealing off the Mediterranean, he could interfere with Britain's communications with the Far East.

The German navy, because of its doubts about an invasion of Britain, favored such a strategy, and Hitler also liked it because it offered a chance to build up a position in northwest Africa and the Atlantic for a future war against the United States. Hitler also entertained the idea of forming a so-called Continental Bloc against Britain, an alliance system that could include Italy, Vichy France, Spain, and even the Soviet Union. In the end, though, none of these plans worked out, in large part because Germany's supposed allies Benito Mussolini, Philippe Pétain, and Francisco Franco would not cooperate in the Führer's grand designs. Pétain and Franco presented Hitler with mutually conflicting demands, while Mussolini, whose help with a Mediterranean strategy would be crucial, launched disastrous campaigns in North Africa and Greece that eventually embroiled the Germans without offering the prospect of a clear and rapid victory.

Even while Hitler considered all these various ways to attack Great Britain and its interests, he was also mulling over another strategy altogether. As early as 23 June he told von Brauchitsch that if Britain were to stay in the war, it would do so in hopes of eventual support from the United States and the USSR. Eliminate the USSR, he believed, and the United States would have to drop out too, to deal with Japanese expansion in the Far East, and Britain would then be defenseless. With Britain powerless to attack in the west for the time being, there seemed little danger in opening up a second front, especially if victory in the east could come quickly. Conquering the Soviet Union would also give Germany huge quantities of additional resources with which to prosecute the war against Britain and, eventually, the United States. And of course, the destruction of the Soviet Union remained one of Hitler's fundamental goals in any case. On 21 July he told the army to start considering an attack on the Soviets, perhaps as early as that autumn. (At that point, actually, von Brauchitsch was already able to present a draft plan; he and Halder did not want to be caught flat-footed, as they had immediately after the unexpectedly rapid fall of France, and they also may have wanted to shape future budget debates.) On

31 July Hitler changed the deadline to the following spring, so that the Wehrmacht could win the campaign in one season. As summer changed to fall and his other options fell away one by one, the attack on the Soviet Union became his main focus. By late autumn, with the invasion of Great Britain on indefinite hold and other operations showing no prospect of quick success, the Führer had made up his mind. On 18 December he issued the first directive for the attack in the east, which he code-named Operation *Barbarossa*. The directive called for the Wehrmacht to destroy the bulk of the Russian army in western Russia and to prevent the withdrawal of significant forces to the interior. Ultimately Hitler wanted his forces to 'erect a barrier against Asiatic Russia' along a line stretching roughly from Archangel to the Volga. That line would be far enough east to prevent the Soviet air forces from being able to reach Germany, while allowing the Luftwaffe to destroy the last Soviet industries in the Urals. Preparations were to be complete by 15 May 1941.[1]

After the war, many of the surviving generals maintained that they viewed Hitler's decision with deep misgivings. They could hardly believe, they claimed, that the Führer would commit them to another two-front conflict, after Germany's disastrous experience in the First World War. Halder criticized Hitler for having underestimated Russian strength and complained that his protests about the 'complete inadequacy' of the information on the Soviet Union went unanswered.[2] He and von Brauchitsch did apparently question the operation on strategic grounds at the time; they believed that Germany would be better off if it maintained friendly relations with the USSR, and they doubted that success in the east would lead to a British surrender. Some officers thought nervously of Napoleon's invasion in 1812, which led to the loss of nearly his entire army.

To the extent that we can believe their postwar statements, some of the generals did display a certain amount of strategic foresight, and Hitler certainly deserves the blame for the fundamental decision to attack, since he bore ultimate responsibility for strategic decision making. With that said, however, we have to view the generals' accounts with skepticism. There is no doubt that they shared Hitler's attitudes toward the 'Jewish–Bolshevik' state and believed that conflict with the USSR was both necessary and inevitable, even if they differed with him on the timing. They also bear some responsibility for Hitler's decision to attack, in that he based his decision in part on the idea that the campaign in the USSR would be quick and easy – and this was a viewpoint that the generals encouraged wholeheartedly. Overall, the generals' postwar protestations ring hollow.

Planning the Military Campaign

Germany's military leaders held to a view of the Soviet Union that comprised two seemingly contradictory faces. On the one hand, Russia had long appeared to them as a standing threat to the peoples of the west, a threat that the political philosophy of Bolshevism only intensified. On the other hand, Russia also appeared to be a 'colossus with feet of clay': politically unstable, filled with disaffected minorities, ineffectively ruled, and militarily weak. The regime there would undoubtedly collapse at the first good blow, they believed. Recent history favored that impression. The Germans had defeated Russia in the First World War, after all. They also had the chance to observe Soviet forces during the civil war in Spain, in the invasion of Poland in 1939, and in the Soviets' 1940 war with Finland. In all those cases Soviet performance had been poor. That poor performance, the Germans surmised, was partly the inevitable result of the political purges that Stalin had carried out in 1937 and 1938, in which between twenty and twenty-five thousand officers, including most of the senior commanders, died. A fair amount of racism also colored the officers' views: they tended to share Hitler's opinion that the Soviet Union was a state of Slavs dominated by Jews, which could hardly be expected to field an effective force. In comparison with the French, whom the Wehrmacht had just defeated with such apparent ease, the Red Army seemed an easy target. Most generals agreed with Hitler that 'a campaign against Russia would be a sand-table exercise in comparison [with the western campaign].'[3]

The planning for the invasion went forward in this optimistic atmosphere during the latter half of 1940. After 21 July, when Hitler made his intentions plain, von Brauchitsch set his planners to work. By the beginning of autumn the staff had come up with its basic campaign plan, which it finalized in late January 1941. It consisted of three rapid thrusts by a total of four armored groups, made up primarily of armored and motorized divisions, backed up by seven slower infantry armies. (Contrary to popular belief, most of the German army still relied on foot infantry and horse-drawn artillery and transport.) The main weight of the attack would move north of the Pripet Marshes, a nearly impassable area of roughly twenty-eight thousand square miles in the center of the western Soviet Union. Army Group North would advance through the Baltic states with Leningrad as its objective, while Army Group Center would head straight for the political capital, rail hub, and industrial center at Moscow, via Minsk and Smolensk. South of the Pripet, meanwhile, Army Group South would aim for Kiev and the rich agricultural and industrial resources of the Ukraine. Each thrust was to penetrate the Soviet defenses as quickly as possible on a narrow front, drive deep into the rear, cut off the Soviet armies, and destroy them. Victory would depend upon the Wehrmacht catching the Red Army as far to the west as possible, before it could withdraw into the interior of the continent and prolong the campaign indefinitely. With that accomplished, the Germans expected that the political structure of the Soviet Union would dissolve.

The General Staff calculated that the campaign would take place in two stages. The initial lunge would take them three-quarters of the way to Leningrad in the north, to Smolensk in the center, and to Kiev in the south. At that point the armies would have to stop, consolidate their lines of communication, replenish the combat units' stocks of supplies, and repair vehicles and equipment before moving on to the main objectives. The planners believed that the armies could complete the entire operation in eleven to fourteen weeks, including the three-week replenishment phase, after which they expected no further organized resistance. That meant that if the invasion began in late May – the original target date – the operation would be over by early September, long before winter snows threatened. At no point did the senior leaders express any doubts about the feasibility of the plan. They had already concluded that the Soviets possessed neither the operational skill to carry out a fighting retreat nor the reserves they would need to continue the fight if they lost their western armies.

Why were the German planners so confident and yet, in the end, so wrong? These were not stupid men, and they possessed years of military experience and training. They believed that they had examined all the possibilities and that their conclusions were valid. In the end, though, they were actually committing one of the greatest acts of hubris in military history. In part, that fact came about because of their broad prejudices concerning the Soviet Union's political stability, military ability, and racial worth. In part it was also the result of a military intelligence system, and a broader military staff system, that contained deep flaws.

The German General Staff, that is, both the army's central operational command element and the elite group that dominated the German officer corps, paid a great deal of attention to the intelligence function. Their manuals emphasized its importance, and their staff structure contained departments whose only job was to collect and assess information on foreign countries and their militaries. Systems existed to ensure that information from many different sources would flow into the system, be evaluated, and then flow out again in condensed form to the people who needed it. To all appearances the system was an efficient one. The main problem with it, however, concerned not the quantity or even the quality of the information, but the ability of the high command to draw the right conclusions from it.

Actually there were two aspects to that problem. One was a subtle but pervasive bias against the intelligence function itself, a bias that

intelligence officers themselves shared. In the Wehrmacht, the process of planning a campaign revolved around the operational concept,
that is, the design by which large forces – armies and army groups –
would move and engage the enemy in the course of a campaign (see
appendix 1 for a diagram of the levels of command). That was the
General Staff's particular area of expertise, the basis for its reputation.
Naturally the Germans considered intelligence to be an important
contributor to the operational concept – but only secondarily. The
role of intelligence was to determine what the Wehrmacht would
face when it carried out the plan of campaign, rather than to shape
that plan to best advantage: in other words, the planners drew up the
plan first, then tried to figure out the enemy's situation and intentions. Moreover, intelligence officers (who received, by the way, no
special training) were clearly subordinate to operations officers in
both rank and position, and so they often had difficulty asserting
their point of view on those occasions when they and the operations officers disagreed. These practices stood in contrast to the
British and American armies, in which intelligence and operations
officers were at least nominally equal in status, and in which intelligence formed part of the basis by which staffs formulated their
plans.

The other major problem within the Germans' intelligence system (though it was certainly not unique to theirs) was a tendency
to accept convenient preconceptions in place of hard facts, especially when intelligence officers had to look beyond the operational
level at issues of politics, economics, and culture. The planning for
Operation *Barbarossa* highlights this weakness. The leading figures
in the OKH lacked complete, accurate information on the Soviet
Union. The Soviets shadowed German embassy personnel constantly
and prevented them from gathering much material. Germany's half-
hearted efforts to insert agents into Stalinist Russia failed. Aerial
reconnaissance revealed only what was visible within a limited distance from the border. And Soviet radio discipline cut down on the
amount of information available through signal intercepts. All this

left the Germans with little more than general impressions, which they consistently interpreted to their own benefit, in the light of their long-standing prejudices.

In August 1940, as the planning process was getting under way, the Germans estimated the Red Army's strength at 221 large units (infantry and cavalry divisions and mechanized brigades), of which 143 would be available in the west to resist an attack by 147 German divisions. By May 1941 the estimate of Soviet forces in the west would rise to 192 major units. The Germans dismissed the forces that the Soviets had in the Far East, because they believed that the threat from Japan would keep them there. All of their intelligence reports emphasized that the Red Army was incapable of conducting a war of movement on a large scale or of withdrawing into the interior, while the planners believed that the presence of so many valuable economic assets in the western part of the country would force the Soviets to defend there. The Wehrmacht's qualitative superiority, the reports concluded, would allow it to defeat the Red Army in the west, and in short order.

These assessments were flawed in several ways. First, they vastly underestimated the USSR's military potential, including the number of units available, the quantity and quality of their equipment, and the skill and flexibility of the officer corps. The OKH's January 1941 estimate that the Soviet Union had two million men under arms was low – by a factor of two. The Red Army had between twenty and twenty-five thousand tanks, not the ten thousand that the Germans expected. Most of them were inferior models, but the T-34 was just coming into production, and it was better than anything the Wehrmacht possessed. Also, while the Germans undercounted the number of Soviet units, they overestimated the number of those units that were in the western border regions by 30 to 50 per cent, so the task of enveloping and destroying the Red Army far to the west would be more difficult than the planners estimated. Taken together, these facts made the German plan to defeat the Soviets in one season extremely problematic.

There were broader analyses that should have called the whole operation into question. On 10 August 1940, for example, the Military Geography Branch of the General Staff issued a report that confirmed Leningrad, Moscow, and the Ukraine as the most valuable targets. It also pointed to the Caucasus, with its oil reserves, as another key goal, but one that was probably beyond Germany's reach in the initial campaign. Then it went on to say, however, that even if the Wehrmacht captured all those areas, victory would still not be certain. Asiatic Russia was no longer a wilderness, the report emphasized: it contained forty million inhabitants, a good railway network, agriculture, and a large per centage of the USSR's industry and raw materials. The study also pointed out that space and climate presented serious obstacles to any attack.

Although the planners had this report early on, however, there is no evidence that it greatly affected their plan, and it certainly made no difference to the basic decision to invade, which became final weeks later without any apparent reference to the report at all. A few lonely souls at the junior staff levels dared to ask what would happen if the Soviets refused to give up; they were told not to worry. The senior commanders were all confident that their armies would defeat the Soviets quickly and that the Soviet regime would then collapse and leave the Germans in firm control of as much territory as they might want. They dismissed any information that called the first premise into question. As for the expectation that the Soviet regime would collapse, the generals could only base that upon the broadest assumptions – assumptions that are interesting indeed, com-ing from men who served a totalitarian regime themselves. The fact was that the Germans went forward despite a general lack of good information about their enemy, and in the face of some facts that should have called their plan into question.

As if the intelligence situation were not bad enough, the Wehrmacht also faced serious logistical and personnel problems, which arose from flaws at several levels. In terms of strategy, the period of indecision and conflicting priorities in 1940, combined with the assumption that the eastern campaign would be easy, left the Germans unprepared for the invasion at the macro level. In July 1940, having defeated France, and with his attention on Britain and America, Hitler had authorized a shift in armaments production to favor the air force and the navy. He also planned to reduce the size of the army and put the men back into the workforce. The decision to launch a massive land campaign in the east forced changes to those priorities and created problems at the same time. Delays resulted from the fact that German industry could not simply turn from tanks to ships to tanks again at the drop of a hat, especially considering that badly needed workers would now remain in the army. Additionally, the German leaders' conviction that the campaign against the USSR would be quick and easy brought with it a level of complacency in their economic planning. As a result they neither took steps to reorganize armaments production nor continued the development of weapons that might prove necessary for a war in the east.

Other problems arose from fundamental flaws in the Germans' staff system. The primacy of the operational concept held true here, as it did with intelligence: typically, the planners created the scheme of maneuver first, then called in the (more junior) supply officers and told them to make sure the supplies got through. That approach worked well enough in France, which was relatively small and possessed good road and railroad networks. The USSR was another matter entirely. There the Wehrmacht had to plan for a force of two million men, with three hundred thousand horses and five hundred thousand vehicles. The distances involved were vast: the Germans' objectives were between six and nine hundred miles from their start lines, and the pace at which the army would have to advance in order to cut off and destroy the Red Army in the west, as the plan dictated, was such that the forward, motorized units would quickly outrun their supply organizations (as well as the mass of the infantry divisions, which moved on foot and depended primarily on horse-drawn transport). The railroads were of a different gauge than those in western Europe, meaning that the Germans would have to rebuild them before they could be of use. To make up the distance, the army would depend mostly upon trucks, but these were in short supply and consisted of a bewildering array of models, which complicated efforts to keep them running. Moreover, the road network in Russia was extremely poor: there were fewer than half as many major arteries as German plans normally called for, and most of them were unpaved. In addition, the Wehrmacht faced shortages of men, munitions, equipment, and fuel, especially given the scope of the task at hand. Some planners forecast that rubber tires and gasoline would run short as early as July, that by October the supply of trained replacement soldiers would run out, and that the army was starting the campaign with a serious shortage of officers.

The Germans' reaction to this situation was a mixture of improvisation and denial. They came up with creative ways to push supplies as far forward as possible, and scraped together every truck they could lay their hands on, from every corner of Germany and occupied Europe. They also dictated that the army would have to live off the land, so that supply priority could go to fuel and ammunition. They filled officer slots with reservists and First World War veterans whom they had recalled to active duty. And when they had done all they could, they simply told themselves that everything would work out. At no time, apparently, did any of the planners question the feasibility of the campaign. In fact, as the challenges facing the Germans became more apparent, they reacted by shortening the amount of time they believed they would need to complete the campaign. The initial estimate was for a campaign of eight to eleven weeks, plus a three-week pause in the middle to rest and resupply. By December 1940 that estimate had shrunk to between eight and eleven weeks including the pause. By April 1941 von Brauchitsch was predicting a tough battle on the frontiers, lasting up to four weeks, after which resistance would be negligible.

By the spring of 1941, the assumption of a short campaign had turned into an obligation, if the invasion was to succeed at all. If the Soviets did not collapse, the Wehrmacht was going to find itself in a winter campaign for which it had not prepared and did not possess sufficient strength. The plan to fulfill that obligation, though, rested on a bed of sketchy information and broad biases. With the clarity of hindsight, we can see that Operation *Barbarossa* was an enormous gamble – and the odds did not favor the attackers.

The economic aspects of the invasion plan deserve some further attention here, because they would have a profound effect both on the course of military operations and on the nature of the occupation regime. Economic planning had been a part of the process from the start; after all, one of Hitler's reasons for invading the Soviet Union was to acquire its vast resources of food and raw materials to support the German war effort. General Georg Thomas, head of the War Economy and Armaments Office in the *Oberkommando der Wehrmacht* (Armed Forces High Command, or OKW), started gathering Russia specialists and forming plans as early as August 1940. His efforts received a boost in November, when Hermann Göring, acting under Hitler's orders, told Thomas to prepare a study on the economic exploitation of the Soviet Union. (Göring, as Plenipotentiary of the Four-Year Plan, played a significant role in economic planning.) Thomas had access to several good studies on Soviet resources and industrial capacity, including the one that the General Staff's Military Geography Branch had prepared. The upshot of those studies was that an invasion would be, at best, of little economic benefit for Germany, and could be a significant risk. Thomas, however, knew that Hitler did not want to hear such pessimistic forecasts, so his study, which he submitted in February 1941, was a good deal more positive: he forecast that Germany would gain enough foodstuffs to satisfy all its import requirements for 1941 and 1942, as well as capturing, intact, 75 per cent of Soviet industry.

Thomas's study was significant in a couple of ways. First, it bolstered Hitler's side in a debate that was just then taking shape between him and the OKH over the operational objectives for the campaign. In the course of planning the attack, Halder and his staff had realized that the army's forces might not have the strength to take Leningrad, Moscow, and the Ukraine simultaneously. Halder believed that Moscow was the key to victory; he believed that the Soviets would deploy their best armies to defend it, and that, therefore, an operation to encircle and capture the city would destroy the last effective forces that might remain after the initial battles in the western part of the country. A staff exercise in early December indicated that such an operation would succeed only if the northern and southern army groups supported the attack in the center, rather than pursuing their own objectives. When Halder presented these findings to Hitler on 5 December however, the Führer countered with a very different concept for the campaign, one in which Moscow assumed less importance, largely for economic reasons. The two men parted without resolving the conflict, or even really acknowledging it. Hitler's concept would reappear in his 18 December directive, while Halder quietly shaped the plan of operations around his ideas. This was the beginning of a battle of wills that would last through the summer and echo even to the present day. In the meantime, Thomas's study would add fuel to the fire by pressing for far-flung operational objectives, including the Ukraine and even the Caucasus.

Thomas's work would also be significant for occupation policy. Previous studies, which had looked at the Germans' experience in the First World War, had concluded that Germany would not be able to extract significant amounts of surplus food from the Soviet Union, especially since the population of the Ukraine had increased markedly since 1918. Thomas, on the other hand, working closely with State Secretary Herbert Backe of the Reich Food Ministry, concluded that Germany could gain millions of tons of grain along with other foodstuffs. The Russian population, he stated, could easily spare the food, since 'the Russian is used to adjusting his consumption to bad harvests.'[4] We do not know if Thomas really believed that, or if he was displaying the uncaring cynicism that so many senior German leaders shared. In any case, the policies that would emerge from Thomas's initial work would have grave consequences for countless Soviet citizens.

Shortly after receiving Thomas's study, Hitler appointed Göring to take charge of all economic exploitation measures for the east, and to use Thomas in the process. By May Thomas was ready to establish the Economic Staff East, which combined military and civilian specialists and would maintain close links to the OKW, the OKH, and the major army field commands. There would be an Economic Inspectorate with each army group headquarters, as well as smaller staffs with the armies and the local occupation force commanders. The role of this organization would be to find, control, and allocate all the economic assets in the occupied territories, in order to supply the army and the Reich with their needs. The appearance of centralized authority is deceptive; the Economic Staff and its subunits would come into conflict with other military and civilian authorities on a regular basis, as each entity attempted to pursue its own economic priorities. Only their determination to strip the Soviet Union for the benefit of Germany gave all of them a common goal.

Planning the War of Annihilation

In the past, many histories have treated the Germans' military and economic plans separately from the criminal designs that came into being at the same time, but in reality they were inseparable. The nature of German military operations, the need for – and assumption of – a quick victory, the difficulties of supply and of securing the vast territories through which the supplies would have to flow: these factors were bound up with broader German strategic, political, and economic goals, racist attitudes, and the concept of total war to an even greater extent than had been the case in Poland. The result would be depredation, suffering, and death on a level nearly unequaled in history.

Germany's senior military leaders could hardly have been surprised at the brutality of the campaign to come. Hitler had expounded several times on the nature of the war in the east, and certainly the events in Poland could have left little doubt in the mind of any astute observer as to the regime's goals and methods. Further indications were not lacking. On 30 March 1941, less than two months before the eastern campaign began, Hitler explained his intentions again, even more explicitly, to the most important commanders and staff officers who would lead the Wehrmacht into the USSR. The war against the Soviet Union would be a war of extermination, he said. Communism was inherently asocial and represented an enormous danger for the future; its leaders were criminals and would have to be dealt with appropriately. The usual rules would not apply. The concept of comradeship among soldiers would have to be discarded. The Bolshevik commissars and intelligentsia would be eliminated, and no new intellectual class would be allowed to rise. Harshness today would mean leniency in the future; if Germany did not defeat the enemy now, he might arise again in thirty years. Hitler was enjoining his audience to violate accepted rules and laws of warfare, as the officers present well knew, but they either accepted the speech at face value or, at any rate, chose not to express their objections too strongly. Von Brauchitsch had, in fact, already told the senior commanders on 27 March that the troops 'have to realize that this struggle is being waged by one race against another, and proceed with the necessary harshness.'[5] The message from the top was clear.

What, exactly, did von Brauchitsch mean by 'harshness'? It encompassed many things: a plan to starve large portions of the population; rear area 'security measures' that amounted to widespread mass murder; orders to shoot political commissars and other 'undesirables'; the use of forced labor on a massive scale; and criminal negligence toward prisoners of war. Absolute ruthlessness was the rule by which the Germans intended to conquer and 'pacify' their new realm.

Perhaps the most cynical of the Germans' plans is also the least well known; it concerned food supplies. Not only would the army's logistical apparatus be unable to bring food forward to the troops in sufficient quantities, but the Reich Food Ministry was also worried about food shortages in Germany itself. Arguments of 'military necessity' now combined with concerns about civilian morale; obviously the troops had to eat, and no one wanted to see a repetition of the hunger and unrest that had weakened home-front morale in the First World War. Over the longer term, as well, Hitler wanted the resources of eastern Europe and European Russia to support an extended conflict with Britain and, in all likelihood, the United States. As a result, representatives of the regime and the military met and, in early May 1941, agreed upon what historians have come to call the 'hunger plan.' According to this plan, the Germans would take the 'surplus' food from the more agriculturally productive southern regions of the USSR to feed the Wehrmacht's troops and the Reich. 'Surplus,' in this context, referred to food that normally went to feed people in the cities and the USSR's less productive northern zone. By agreeing to this plan, German military and civilian authorities quietly accepted that up to thirty million Soviet citizens would starve to death – not because they had done anything wrong or represented any threat, but simply because the Germans believed that their needs trumped other people's.

Other measures aimed to ensure security and promote Nazi racial goals in the occupied territories by actively eliminating partisans, potential partisans, and anyone else whom the Germans saw as a near- or long-term threat to their overlordship. These policies grew from two overlapping imperatives: that of the military, which did not want problems in the rear areas to slow its advance, and that of the civilian authorities, who needed to maintain strict control in order to exploit the conquered lands and who also wanted to eliminate Jews and other supposedly inferior people outright, as a matter of principle.

Hitler began laying the groundwork for these measures early in 1941. Jodl had presented him with a draft administrative plan for the areas behind the front in December 1940, but he rejected its provisions as too traditional; the plan called for military administration over all the conquered territory, and he did not fully trust the army to carry out his political plans. According to his alternative concept, the army would control only the narrowest possible band of territory behind the front. Behind that, a series of large regions would be under the control of Reich Commissars, that is, civilian political appointees who would each be responsible for setting up a new state (*Reichskommissariat*) under German control. Hitler also stated that Himmler and the army would have to consider whether or not the SS should have forces operating with the army's Secret Field Police within the zone of operations, in order to eliminate Bolshevik officials and commissars. And he expressed his wish that the army restrict the jurisdiction of military courts to purely internal affairs.

Accordingly, over the next three months the OKW, the OKH, and the SS worked out a series of plans and orders that corresponded to Hitler's wishes. One of these, which the OKW issued on 13 March as a supplement to the basic order for *Barbarossa*, delineated the respective spheres of responsibility for the army and the SS, in general terms. It stated that Hitler had given the *Reichsführer*-SS (Himmler) certain 'special tasks,' tasks that 'arise from the final struggle between two opposing political systems,' and that Himmler would deal with 'independently and on his own authority.'[6] Negotiations began that very same day between Wagner and Heydrich (by now the head of the SS Main Office for Reich Security, which controlled the Security Police and SD) on the nature of army-SS cooperation. Records of their meetings do not exist, but we can assume that the talks went smoothly, since a draft agreement was ready on 26 March and von Brauchitsch signed the resulting order on 28 April. According to this order, 'special detachments' of the Security Police and SD would carry out 'special tasks' within the army's zone of operations, tasks that would fall outside the jurisdiction of the troops. Although the order did not name them as such, these 'special detachments' were the SS *Einsatzgruppen*, the same kinds of units that had carried out 'special tasks' in Poland. The detachments would act on their own responsibility, taking their operational instructions from Heydrich, but would coordinate closely with the army units in whose areas they operated. The army would determine their line of march as well as providing supplies and accommodations. Their mission included 'securing ... important individuals (leading émigrés, saboteurs, terrorists, etc.).'[7] No preinvasion written order with any mention of liquidations has surfaced, and after the war Halder and other senior officers would claim that they did not know what the *Einsatzgruppen* were going to do. However, given the groups' activities in Poland, and especially in light of the other orders that the military was preparing at this time, that claim is nearly impossible to credit.

Any lingering squeamishness notwithstanding, the army's leaders saw the *Einsatzgruppen* as a valuable addition to their security apparatus, as they had in Poland. Even considering the limitations that Hitler placed upon its sphere of authority, the army still would have vast territories to control. In order to do so, the OKH divided the area into three zones that extended rearward from the front line. The first was the combat zone: the area where the fighting was actually taking place and the land immediately behind it. This zone would be under the control of the division and corps headquarters. Next came the army rear areas, each of which lay behind the combat zones for an army's subordinate corps. Finally, there were three army group rear areas behind those for the armies. Each rear area would have its own headquarters that would report to the corresponding army or army group commander and also take direction from Wagner, who would be responsible for rear area security overall.

In addition to the *Einsatzgruppen*, whose subordinate units had received authorization to operate in the army and army group rear areas (and would actually follow close behind the combat units from the start of the campaign), the army group rear area commanders also controlled Security Divisions and units of the Secret Field Police. Moreover, on 21 May Himmler appointed a Higher SS and Police Leader for each army group's rear area. These men would exercise direct control over the *Einsatzgruppen* and would also each have a police regiment and units of Order Police with which to support the operations of the Security Divisions. All told, these additional units would come to outnumber the *Einsatzgruppen* severalfold. All of this was good news for the army's leaders, who above all else wanted to ensure that the lines of communication to the front remained open and that the occupied territories yielded the required quantities of food, fodder, other materials, and labor. If that meant rough treatment for Jews and Slavs, most of whom the officers assumed to be Bolsheviks in any case, most commanders would not protest, so long as such actions did not threaten discipline. The euphemistic language in von Brauchitsch's order was perhaps a way of avoiding the harsh realities, but it did not change them, or his and other officers' awareness of them.

Fewer euphemisms were evident in a series of orders that dealt directly with the treatment of enemy civilians. On 3 April Wagner issued a supplementary order entitled 'Special Instructions on Supplies, Part C,' in which he enjoined the troops to suppress any resistance with the utmost brutality: 'Self-assured and ruthless behavior towards anti-German elements will prove an effective preventive means.' The order also regulated the treatment of POWs, which was to be proper, but with the proviso that the troops had to be on the alert for insidious behavior: 'Total liquidation of any active or passive resistance!'[8] And as we shall see, the concept of 'proper' treatment would soon fall victim to that of 'military necessity,' with assistance from Nazi ideology.

Another order, this one dated 13 May and entitled 'Decree on the Exercise of Military Jurisdiction in the 'Barbarossa' Zone and on Special Measures for the Troops,' provided still broader guidance. This one was an outgrowth of Hitler's desire to limit military courts' jurisdiction to internal military matters, and several high-ranking military figures, including Jodl and Halder, took part in its formulation. The decree began by saying that the shortage of personnel and the 'special nature' of the enemy meant that the troops would have to defend themselves 'mercilessly' against any threat from the civilian population. It went on to stipulate that civilians accused of crimes would not be tried by military courts; that 'guerillas are to be finished off ruthlessly in battle or while attempting to escape'; and that all other attacks by civilians were to be 'crushed by the troops on the spot using the utmost means, until the attacker is annihilated.' Those civilians whom the troops merely suspected of an offense were to be brought before an officer, who would decide whether or not they were to be shot. Where individual offenders could not be identified, 'collective measures' could be taken against a locality from which an attack came, with the approval of a battalion commander or higher. Furthermore, there was no obligation to prosecute a member of the Wehrmacht for crimes committed against civilians, even if such crimes constituted offenses against military law. If authorities did prosecute such actions, they were to take into account the 'fact' that Bolshevism had contributed to the collapse of 1918, the subsequent sufferings of the German people, and the National Socialist movement's bloody losses. Although von Brauchitsch issued an order on 24 May that modified the decree somewhat, the new version clearly aimed at maintaining military discipline and did not otherwise interfere with Hitler's intent. In effect, the highest German authorities all but gave their soldiers carte blanche to abuse Soviet civilians. And just to make sure that the men got the point, on 19 May the OKW also issued a document entitled 'Guidelines for the Behavior of Troops in Russia.' The battle against Bolshevism, it stated, 'demands ruthless and energetic action against Bolshevik agitators, saboteurs, and Jews, and the total elimination of all active or passive resistance.' It then went on to warn the troops, among other things, to watch out for enemy agents and to exercise the greatest care when dealing with POWs, especially those of Asian origin, whom it called 'devious, unpredictable, underhanded and unfeeling.'

Subordinate headquarters often added their own versions of such directives. On 16 June the headquarters of Seventeenth Army told its troops that they could expect 'treacherous and sadistic' conduct from the Soviets, in part because of Asiatic influences and in part because of the Soviet Union's 'Bolshevik-Jewish leadership.'[9] And at the beginning of May, General Erich Hoepner of Armored Group 4 issued an order to his troops that said in part:

[The war against Russia] is the old fight of the Germans against the Slavs, the defense of European culture against the Moscovite-Asiatic flood, the repulsion of Jewish Bolshevism. The goal of this fight must be the destruction of contemporary Russia and therefore must be conducted with enormous violence. Every combat action, in its conception and conduct, must be governed by the iron will to pitiless and complete annihilation of the enemy. In particular there is no mercy for the carriers of the current Russian-Bolshevik system.[10]

One other directive was perhaps the most explicit preinvasion statement of the Germans' intentions in their fight against the 'Jewish-Bolshevik' enemy: the 'Guidelines for the Treatment of Political Commissars,' which the OKW issued on 6 June, based on an OKH draft. The political commissars were uniformed members of the Soviet military who occupied positions parallel to those of unit commanders. Their job was to indoctrinate the troops and ensure that the commanders' decisions reflected appropriate loyalty to the Soviet state. The Germans considered the commissars to be the core of the Communist military system and the 'originators of barbaric Asiatic fighting methods'; their elimination would make the conquest of the east that much easier and would also help with the control of POWs by preventing the spread of Bolshevik propaganda in the camps.[11] For those reasons the so-called Commissar Order called on front-line troops to immediately shoot any commissars they captured. This order constituted a clear violation of international laws to which Germany was a signatory, but it aroused no protest on the part of the senior commanders when they heard of it, aside from some concerns, again, about troop discipline. Halder's comment when he first saw a draft of the order was that the troops 'must do their share in the ideological struggle of the eastern campaign.'[12] The order went in writing to the two most senior levels in the chain of command below the OKH – the army group and army headquarters – with instructions to pass it on verbally from there; from that last stipulation we can judge that the Wehrmacht's leaders were aware of the illegality of their orders.

Prisoners of war were another major concern. The military leaders knew that if the plan of operations was successful, large numbers of Soviet soldiers – between one and two million – would fall into the Wehrmacht's hands within six or eight weeks. Caring for them would be no simple task. By the time Wagner issued his order of 3 April, preparations had been going on for some time in higher headquarters. Overall policy was, technically, the responsibility of the POW Branch of the OKW's General Armed Forces Office (*Allgemeine Wehrmachtamt*, or AWA). However, the head of the AWA, General Hermann Reinecke, maintained personal control over most POW policies relating to Operation *Barbarossa*. He, his staff, and a series of regional commanders and headquarters controlled POW affairs within the so-called OKW zone in the rear, while the OKH controlled them in its zone through a similar set of commanders and staffs. According to the early plans, any prisoners whom the army did not put to work would move from division-level holding areas to larger collection points in the army rear areas, then to transit camps in the army group rear areas, all within the OKH POW zone. From there the OKW would take over, and the prisoners would move on to reception sites near the USSR's western borders, in East Prussia and the General Government (that eastern part of occupied Poland that the Germans did not annex), then to clearing stations farther west, and finally to camps in Germany proper: Stalags for enlisted men and Oflags for officers. The idea, at least initially, was to move the prisoners through this system as rapidly as possible, so as not to overburden the supply system at the front.

After the war, some former Wehrmacht generals tried to maintain that this system broke down and prisoners died because of the unexpectedly large number of captives, the duration of the campaign, and the failure of the supply and transport systems. Actually, the sufferings of the Soviet prisoners had more to do with Wehrmacht negligence than fate. General Reinecke had strong National Socialist sympathies, and he viewed the fate of Soviet prisoners accordingly. He was not alone. In the preinvasion planning and throughout the

Russo-German war, Soviet prisoners would occupy the lowest level of a POW hierarchy in which the Americans and British would be on top, followed by the other western nationalities – French, Norwegians, Belgians, and Dutch – then prisoners from the Balkans, and then the Poles. This hierarchy developed in part out of considerations of race and in part out of a calculation of which countries might be able to threaten German POWs with retribution. Those at the bottom of the hierarchy were, for all intents and purposes, threatened with extinction.

The Germans' intentions for their Soviet prisoners became clear at the latest on 16 June when the OKW issued an order governing their treatment. The order parroted much of what the other orders had said: that Bolshevism was Germany's mortal enemy; that dealing with any Russian soldiers, especially Asians, called for the utmost watchfulness; and that any active or passive resistance was to be put down ruthlessly. It also pointed out that the Soviet Union was not a signatory to the 1929 Geneva convention on the handling of POWs, but went on to claim that the convention would govern German actions. Such a claim was only proper; signatories to the convention are not released from their obligations just because their opponent is not a party to the treaty. The convention requires the holding power to keep prisoners in houses or barracks that are properly heated and ventilated; to provide bedding and food of the same quantity and quality as that provided to the holding power's own replacement troops; to supply the prisoners with clothing and shoes; and to ensure adequate hygienic conditions and medical care. The holding power may put prisoners to work, but not in support of the war effort, and may only discipline them in the same way as it disciplines its own troops. Corporal punishment is forbidden. The 16 June order called for the violation of two of those provisions outright: it stated that Soviet prisoners would work in direct support of German troops, and it stipulated that disciplinary measures would not be subject to Red Cross restrictions. It also called for the prisoners to be cut off from any aid: their names would not be reported to the Red Cross, and they would be allowed no contact with any aid organization or protective power. A special order on feeding them, it said, would follow later.

Food would remain a key issue, and given the Germans' willingness to starve up to thirty million civilians, one can hardly expect that the POWs would fare much better. Wagner's 3 April order had stated that those prisoners who were willing to work were to receive 'sufficient food.' That was bound to be a problem, however, in territory in which the Wehrmacht was living off the land and sending foodstuffs to Germany. In late May and early June a number of army-level headquarters issued instructions to the effect that the prisoners were to receive only the poorest quality food, and not much of that. The caloric intake that some orders specified was actually below the minimum necessary for survival. In the meantime, local authorities in the General Government and East Prussia had begun preparing the reception sites for incoming prisoners, and those preparations also demonstrated, at best, a lack of concern for the prisoners' welfare. Records indicate that the sites consisted of nothing more than large areas that the Germans fenced in. They built no barracks and made few or no provisions for sanitation or feeding. Such amenities might not have been too important if the Germans had shipped the prisoners back to camps farther in the rear right away. However, the 16 June order from the OKW stipulated that Soviet prisoners not be shipped from the reception sites to Germany, but rather that they be held, up to the absolute maximum capacity of the camps, until the OKW ordered otherwise. Taken together, these orders amounted to a recipe for massive casualties among Soviet prisoners.

With the clarity of hindsight, we can see that the German plan to conquer the Soviet Union contained the seeds of its own failure. The nature of the Nazi regime and its military planners' modes of thought were such that we can hardly expect them to have come up with a better set of ideas or even to grasp the flaws in the ones they did develop. Germany's leaders were, like people throughout history, the products of their time and place. They controlled an army that had defeated the best in the world with apparent ease. They had achieved in weeks a victory that had eluded them for years in the Great War. They were convinced of their moral, intellectual, and fundamental racial superiority, and they believed they were fighting for their people's very survival, so they held any means to be justifiable in pursuit of victory. They viewed the Soviet Union – with justification – as a corrupt, malevolent force. They believed that the people of the east were inferior, their needs and desires undeserving of consideration except as an afterthought. Such people transferred their inferiority to their military and their government; surely those institutions would prove no great obstacle, and there would be no need to enlist the help of dissident groups in any serious way. All that counted was rapid victory and exploitation, which the Wehrmacht's leaders believed they could achieve easily, provided they were sufficiently ruthless. In the end, such attitudes and plans would doom the Wehrmacht and Germany, along with millions of Soviet citizens, to death and suffering on a scale that none of the generals could have imagined in the spring of 1941, but for which they were directly responsible. Millions of people in the Soviet Union had suffered horribly under the Stalinist regime and wanted desperately to see its end. Many of them were ready to welcome the Germans as liberators. Only a regime such as Hitler's could have persuaded them, through its actions, that life under Stalin was preferable. The stage was now set for that tragedy to play itself out.

3

Initial Victories and Atrocities, June to August

By the morning of 22 June 1941, the Germans had amassed a force of over three million of its own soldiers and another half million of its allies for the start of the invasion. The attack opened at 0315, when a small force of bombers struck key Soviet air bases at the same time that the ground campaign began with an artillery bombardment up and down the long border with the USSR. At dawn, more than 1,200 German aircraft – part of a total force of over 2,700 – crossed the Soviet border and began bombing additional Red Army airfields. They caught most of the Soviet planes on the ground and destroyed hundreds of them before the morning was out. By then the Wehrmacht had begun its advance against light resistance. Operation *Barbarossa*, which would grow into the most destructive military conflict of all time, had begun.

The attack came as a nearly complete surprise to Stalin. When he signed the nonaggression pact with Germany in August 1939, he apparently expected that Germany and the western allies would bleed themselves white in a protracted conflict. Germany's rapid victory over France, and Britain's apparent impotence, came as a rude shock. Over the course of the following months, tensions between Germany and the USSR grew. The latter took control of territory in Lithuania that the Germans considered to be part of their sphere of influence, while Germany, for its part, upset the Soviets with military missions to Finland and the Balkans. On the economic side, the Soviets delivered millions of tons of vital grain and raw materials to the Germans in accordance with their economic agreements, while Germany fell well short on promised deliveries of weapons and other industrial goods to the USSR. By the spring of 1941 the Germans were also quite obviously building up a massive military force in eastern Europe, and both Soviet agents and western governments warned that an attack was coming. For a variety of reasons, though, Stalin was distrustful of such information. He believed that Britain, especially, was perfectly capable of embroiling the Soviet Union in a war with Germany for its own ends. He also feared that excessive military preparations in the western territories, or a cutoff of Soviet goods shipments, could provoke a German attack. Therefore he did everything he could to pacify Germany, even while he accelerated a massive modernization and reorganization of the Soviet military. He tried repeatedly to establish a new agreement with Hitler, and he continued the raw materials deliveries right to the end; the last train moved across the border just hours before the invasion began. He also refused to allow his forces in the western USSR and Poland to deploy for imminent combat, despite increasingly shrill warnings from all quarters, and so most Soviet forces were unready for the Wehrmacht's onslaught.

Military Operations to the Beginning of July

On the northern end of the front, Army Group North under Field Marshal Wilhelm Ritter von Leeb opened the campaign with three armies: Eighteenth Army, under General Georg von Küchler, Armored Group 4 under General Hoepner, and Sixteenth Army under General Ernst Busch. Their sector bordered the Baltic Sea in the north and extended northeast from East Prussia through

Lithuania, Latvia, and Estonia – which the Soviets had recently annexed – to the northern reaches of the Soviet Union around Leningrad (see map 1). The terrain consisted of almost completely flat territory, relatively open in the west but then becoming heavily forested with evergreens, and crisscrossed with major water obstacles such as the Dvina River and Lake Peipus, along with a zone of swampy territory south of Leningrad. The initial operations order called for Hoepner's Armored Group 4, the most mobile of the armies, to establish bridgeheads over the Dvina at Daugavpils and be ready to advance further to the north or northeast. The two slower infantry armies were to follow along to either side as rapidly as possible, protect the armored force's flanks, and mop up units it had bypassed. Eighteenth Army, on the left, was to capture the Dvina crossings southeast of Riga, cut off the Red Army forces west of that river, capture Riga itself, and then be ready to move on Ostrov and Pskov and to clear the western portions of Estonia. Sixteenth Army, on the right, was to cross the Neman at Kaunas and continue on to Daugavpils.

Von Leeb's forces quickly built up momentum that would be impossible for the Soviets to counter. The losses the Luftwaffe inflicted on the Soviet air forces gave the Germans aerial supremacy, and they soon turned their attention to Soviet troop concentrations, rail movements, and command centers. Those strikes, in turn, in addition to radio jamming and deep raids by German commandos, added persistent confusion and disorganization to the effects of the initial surprise. Within a day the Soviets had started fighting hard, confirming the German generals' assumption that the Red Army would defend as far forward as possible, but without a coherent command structure or air protection, they could not hope to resist effectively. Crossings over the border rivers, which could have been serious obstacles, fell to the Wehrmacht intact. Within four days, Hoepner's armored group had captured the Dvina bridges at Daugavpils. Soon the Germans were establishing other crossing points as well. Riga fell by 1 July, by which time the infantry had caught up to the tanks and the army group was ready to launch the next phase of the operation. Von Leeb could look upon his progress to date with satisfaction, and his army group was also in better shape logistically than the other two, both because it had captured significant stocks of Soviet material and because it had taken the railways and bridges in its sector in good condition.

Army Group Center's mission was to advance into Belorussia, past Minsk to Smolensk, in the process destroying Soviet forces in the region, and then to prepare to continue its advance toward Moscow. Its commander, Field Marshal Fedor von Bock, controlled four armies. In the first stage of the invasion, Armored Group 3, under General Hermann Hoth, and Armored Group 2, under General Heinz Guderian, were to form a pair of pincers on the left and right sides of the sector and advance to Minsk, trapping Soviet forces between Minsk and the border in a vast encirclement. Ninth Army on the left, under General Adolf Strauss, and Field Marshal Günther von Kluge's Fourth Army on the right were to follow the two armored groups, protect their flanks, form an inner encirclement east of Bialystok, and then help seal off the larger encirclement around Minsk (see map 1). The terrain in Army Group Center's sector was more open than that farther north, although here too there were major rivers that the armies would have to cross: the Neman and the Bug at first, and later the Berezina, the Dvina, and the Dnieper. The very center of the sector held an especially important feature: a forty-mile-wide gap where a broad, low ridge divided the upper reaches of the Dvina and the Dnieper, leaving the way to Smolensk and Moscow wide open. The Pripet Marshes, through which the boundary between Army Groups Center and South ran, formed a major obstacle, especially to mechanized forces, and offered perfect territory from which Soviet units could fight a guerrilla war. The First Cavalry Division – the German army's only large cavalry formation – would cover that flank.

Here, as in the north, the Wehrmacht caught the Soviets completely by surprise. Armored Group 3 captured bridges over the Neman south of Kaunas and continued east, taking Vilnius on 24

June and then turning southeast toward Minsk. Guderian's forces bypassed the fortress city of Brest-Litovsk and moved on toward Baranovici, approaching Minsk from the southwest. The two groups met and closed the ring at Minsk on 28 June. Fourth and Ninth armies, meanwhile, cut off Soviet forces around Bialystok, but only weakly; elements of the Red Army were able to escape eastward for some days, with the help of otherwise fruitless Soviet counterattacks. Likewise, the infantry armies were unable to keep up with the armored groups, and so the latter's encirclement at Minsk was also imperfect. At the end of the month, von Bock's army group had its hands full trying to contain surrounded Soviet elements and prepare for the next jump forward.

Army Group South, under Field Marshal Gerd von Rundstedt, was to destroy Soviet forces in Galicia and western Ukraine by advancing as rapidly as possible from the area around Lublin to Kiev, crossing the Dnieper there, and then continuing southeast along the river in a single envelopment, thus preventing Soviet forces to the west from escaping (see map 2). To accomplish this, it concentrated three armies along the Polish-Soviet border north and west of Lvov. Armored Group 1 under General Ewald von Kleist, with support from Field Marshal Walter von Reichenau's Sixth Army, would race east for Kiev, while Seventeenth Army under General Carl Heinrich von Stülpnagel pushed southeast past Lvov toward Vinnitsa. Another German army, General Eugen Ritter von Schobert's Eleventh, was to advance northeast out of Romania, together with forces from that nation, to meet Stülpnagel's army in the area around Vinnitsa. Hungary would also join the campaign by sending forces northeast out of its territory. As far as terrain was concerned, there were again significant river obstacles, especially the Bug on the Polish border, the Dniester facing Romania, and the Dnieper. The Pripet Marshes also constituted the same sort of hazard on the army group's northern flank as it did on the south side of Army Group Center. The land was largely flat, with a mix of trees and brush in the northern areas giving way to treeless plains and farm fields in the south.

Unfortunately for Army Group South, the Soviet armies facing it were better prepared than their comrades in other sectors. For one thing, to the extent that the Soviets had planned for a German attack, they expected the main weight of the offensive south of the Pripet, so the Soviet forces there were stronger than in the north. Moreover, the local Soviet commander had risked Stalin's displeasure by ordering some defensive preparations as he saw the situation deteriorating in the weeks before the campaign opened. The German attack met stiff resistance on the Bug, and the Soviets also held on fiercely in front of Lvov, contrary to German expectations. That latter development exposed Armored Group 1's southern flank to a series of Soviet counterattacks that temporarily halted its progress. By 25 June the army group headquarters was already having to consider the possibility that it would not be able to cut off the Soviet forces west of the Dnieper. Only on 27 June did the Soviets begin withdrawing, in good order, from the area around Lvov. The city fell on 30 June, by which time the German leaders were debating the further conduct of the campaign.

German Assessments, and the Next Phase

Despite the setbacks in the southern sector, by early July the mood among Germany's senior political and military leaders was euphoric. Some German units had advanced more than two hundred miles in fewer than ten days of fighting. Soviet losses had been enormous. In Army Group Center's sector alone, the Wehrmacht had killed or captured more than four hundred thousand Red Army soldiers. The Soviet mechanized forces that had been engaged with the Germans had lost 90 per cent of their strength. On 3 July Halder recorded in his diary:

On the whole, then, it may be said even now that the objective to shatter the bulk of the Russian army this side of the Dvina and the Dnieper has been accomplished. I do not doubt ... that east of the Dvina and Dnieper we would encounter nothing more than partial forces. ... It is thus probably no overstatement to say that the Russian campaign has been won in the space of two weeks. Of course, this does not mean that it is closed. The sheer geographical vastness of the country and the stubbornness of the resistance, which is carried on with all means, will claim our efforts for many more weeks to come. ... Once we are across the Dvina and the Dnieper, it will be less a question of smashing enemy armies than of denying the enemy possession of his production centers and so prevent his raising a new army with the aid of his gigantic industrial potential and inexhaustible manpower resources.[1]

On the same day, the General Staff generated a draft plan for the operations to follow *Barbarossa*. The Germans believed that their forces had destroyed more than half of the Soviets' major units, including twenty of twenty-nine armored units, and they assumed that the USSR would be unable to restore its defeated forces' combat effectiveness. Hitler declared, 'To all intents and purposes the Russians have lost the war'; soon thereafter, Jodl and von Brauchitsch began working out the shape of a post-*Barbarossa* army.[2]

In the meantime, however, conflict was increasing between Hitler and his generals over the further conduct of the campaign, on at least two levels. First, Hitler was convinced that the army should use shallow envelopments against Soviet forces and then seal off those pockets and destroy them before moving on. He was the one who insisted upon an encirclement closing at Minsk, rather than at Smolensk, as von Bock, Guderian, and Hoth had all wanted, and his argument had some validity, since the armored forces would have left the infantry far behind and could not possibly have sealed such a large pocket effectively by themselves. The second level of disagreement concerned Army Group Center's operational objectives after it breached the Dvina-Dnieper line. Von Brauchitsch, Halder, von Bock, and their subordinates still wanted to go for Moscow, and assumed, in fact, that such would be their course. Hitler continued to maintain that Moscow was not the most important objective, and that he might divert forces from the center to the north and south. In this developing conflict, von Brauchitsch, even had he possessed the strength of personality to stand up to the Führer, was in no position to do so; his impotence soon began to damage his relations with both his superior and his subordinates. The army group and army commanders had the luxury of distance from the Führer, which allowed them some freedom of expression, but ultimately they could not change the course of events much. Halder was in the middle, and because he had long since learned the futility of confronting Hitler directly, he continued a policy of dissimulation and subterfuge, sidestepping the conflicts but issuing orders and guidance that either ignored Hitler's wishes or merely gave an appearance of agreement while undermining the Führer's intent.

Both sets of disagreements had come up more and more frequently as the campaign had developed. On 25 June – only three days after the invasion began – Hitler sent an order to the OKH in which he expressed his concern that Army Groups Center and South were operating in too much depth. Halder commented, 'The old refrain! But that is not going to change anything in our plans.'[3] Then on 29 June he faced a situation in which he wanted Guderian's forces to move on through Bobruisk to cross the Dnieper at Mogilev and Rogachev, but Hitler was holding those units back to help seal off the Minsk encirclement. Halder was reduced to hoping that 'the [commanding generals] of corps and armies will do the right thing even without express orders, which we are not allowed to issue because of the Führer's instruction to [von Brauchitsch].'[4] And on 3 July Halder complained again of hearing 'the usual rumors' from the Führer headquarters about the threat of Soviet flank attacks, noting, 'What is lacking on top level is that confidence in the executive commands which is one of the most essential features of our command organization.'[5] Halder was in a poor position to speak of trust, however. His attitude, and the obstructionism that followed from it, could only alienate Hitler, who would eventually perceive that the army chief of staff was trying to thwart him, while it also confused the middle-level commanders and encouraged them, in turn, to disregard orders with which they did not agree.

The more long-standing and serious dispute over operational objectives, meanwhile, was beginning to dominate the discussions within the high command. The OKW war diary records that on 27 June Hitler opined that 'it does not matter if we hit the enemy capital, but rather the enemy's forces.'[6] At other times he emphasized the economic importance of Leningrad and the Ukraine. To some extent his generals agreed with him; they knew the importance of those regions and wanted to take them. They simply believed that by attacking Moscow, itself an important industrial center and rail hub, they would also lure the mass of the Red Army to its destruction. By the first week of July Hitler was openly wavering; he called the decision the most difficult of the campaign. On 8 July he met with von Brauchitsch and Halder to discuss the situation. In that meeting, Hitler approved an operational outline that still left the question open. Army Group Center, he agreed, would advance to destroy the bulk of the enemy's forces in the Smolensk-Vitebsk-Orsha triangle, thus opening the most direct and easiest route to Moscow. After that, both armored groups would halt. Hoth might go north at that point to help von Leeb, although Hitler preferred that the latter accomplish his mission with the forces he had at hand. As an alternative, Hoth could drive northeast to envelop Moscow from the north; this was an idea of which Halder could approve unreservedly. On the other side of the sector, Hitler considered sending Guderian south into the eastern Ukraine. Halder's diary contains no hint that he disapproved of that plan, either. Probably he believed that, with the destruction of the Soviet forces near Smolensk, the way to Moscow would be open, and the mobile forces would no longer be needed. Whatever his reasoning, Halder apparently still believed that the attack on Moscow would go forward. On 13 July he briefed Hitler on a plan that corresponded to the Führer's 8 July concept superficially, but that clearly aligned the forces for a drive on the Soviet capital. At the same time, and apparently with Halder's prompting, Bock registered his protest at the idea that Hoth's tanks might be sent north.

The debates at the top soon began to have their effect on operations in the field. On 2 July, Army Group North had directed Armored Group 4 to the northeast into the area between Lake Peipus and Lake Ilmen, via the cities of Ostrov and Pskov (see map 1). Soviet resistance was light and disorganized, and the Germans had little trouble advancing. Within two days Hoepner's tanks reached the old Latvian/Russian border, and on 5 July Ostrov fell. Eighteenth Army began its attack to the left of the armored group on 4 July, while Sixteenth Army did the same on the right flank. On the third, meanwhile, the OKH ordered the army group to prepare to send its mobile forces 180 miles north to Narva, thus cutting off Soviet forces to the west in Estonia, and then to head east for Leningrad, another hundred miles distant. At this point, however, the offensive began to lose its coherence. In the course of the 8 July meeting, Hitler demanded that Hoepner advance through the area of Luga and Novgorod to cut Leningrad off from the south and southeast. Halder and von Leeb both accepted these new orders, presumably because they believed the Soviets in the area were on their last legs – and because, in Halder's case, he desperately wanted to avoid a diversion of additional forces from the drive on Moscow. The new direction, however, would take Hoepner's group into an area of especially dense forests and impassable swamps that would be difficult to negotiate even if the Soviets melted away, which they did not. Resistance stiffened almost immediately upon the resumption of the offensive on 10 July, and within two days Hoepner decided to send part of his armored group around to the left, to attack Leningrad from the area southwest of Luga. By 14 July he had started the new advance, but now his group was split, with part facing Novgorod and Staraya Russa, the other part eighty miles away to the northwest. Strong Soviet counterattacks continued all along the line, and especially on the armored group's southeastern flank, where Sixteenth Army had been unable to keep up. Eighteenth Army had to send a corps to help on Hoepner's right wing, while the rest of von Küchler's force struggled to clear Estonia. By 17 July von Leeb had to recognize that his forces could not do everything at once. He decided to carry out the remaining operations in stages, first reinforcing Sixteenth Army in the east and pushing the enemy there back before launching the main attack with Armored Group 4 from the area between Novgorod and Narva to cut off Leningrad. He ordered Hoepner to hold in place, resupply, and reorganize for a new attack on 25 July, while Busch's forces pushed eastward.

At the end of June in Army Group Center's sector, the armies were trying to simultaneously eliminate the Minsk pocket and prepare for their next move. On 30 June Halder selected 3 July as the date for a drive on Smolensk, even though the infantry and most of the mobile forces were still working to contain and destroy the Soviet armies they had already bypassed (not until 8 July did the Germans finally eliminate the last organized resistance west of Minsk). He reorganized the forces by placing the armored groups under von Kluge's headquarters, now renamed Fourth Armored Army, and putting General Maximilian von Weichs's Second Army headquarters, which had been in reserve, in charge of the units that had comprised Fourth Army, on the army group's southern flank. The mission of Hoth's and Guderian's armored groups would be first to secure the line Rogachev-Mogilev-Orsha-Vitebsk-Polotsk and then to continue the advance north and south of Smolensk, respectively (see map 1). Hoth was also to send some forces in the direction of Nevel. Second Army would follow Armored Group 2 and cover the southern flank, while Ninth Army did the same for Armored Group 3 to the north; their main mission was to secure the land bridge between the Dvina and the Dnieper rivers at Vitebsk and Orsha.

Like von Leeb's thrust to the south of Leningrad, von Bock's new offensive did not go as smoothly as planned. The Germans learned quickly, and to their surprise, that the Soviets had been able to bring up reinforcements. New Soviet units appeared all along the front, and though they were ill equipped, inadequately trained, and often poorly led, they fought a series of desperate defensive actions and counterattacks. The weather also turned hostile: strong summer thunderstorms made roads impassable and put hundreds of vehicles out of action. And there were disagreements and misunderstandings within the German command structure over the objectives of the attack, the goals for the next phase, and the conflicting demands of rapid, deep penetrations versus operations to seal off encircled Soviet forces. The conflicts led to a situation in which the armored spearheads did not act as a concentrated mass, but rather in a series of separate, weaker thrusts, while the infantry armies lagged far behind.

The end result was another German victory, but not the easy, nearly total triumph that the Wehrmacht's leaders had been expecting. Armored Group 3 took Vitebsk on 9 July, but only after going on the defensive near Polotsk in order to concentrate its forces in the center of its sector. Armored Group 2, meanwhile, faced tough resistance in the northern part of its zone; it took Rogachev on July 5 but was unable to take Orsha or Mogilev. On 11 July both groups renewed the offensive, but now with seemingly divergent goals. Hoth focused at first on a drive to the northeast, in which he took Nevel and Velizh by 13 July; he apparently had his eye on Rzhev, as a stepping-stone for further operations north of Moscow. Von Kluge, however, forced him to turn back to the southeast, in accordance with the army group's plan for an encirclement of the Soviet forces near Smolensk. On 16 July Hoth's forces captured Yartsevo, thus forming the northern half of the envelopment. In the south, Guderian had crossed the Dnieper at points south of Orsha and Mogilev and had raced on for Yelna and Roslavl, diverging from Hoth's more northeasterly advance. The Soviets launched massive counterattacks on the southern flank of this operation, as well as from Orsha and Mogilev, on 13 July, and the advance on Roslavl had to be abandoned. The Germans took and held Yelna, however, despite heavy losses, and went on to take Smolensk itself on July 16. From that point the two armored groups and the following infantry armies fought to close the pocket, but because their forces were dispersed they needed another eight days to do so, and two weeks beyond that in order to eliminate it completely. A combination of Soviet resistance, poor weather, and command difficulties had interfered with the operation on several levels. All the same, the Germans were now two hundred miles closer to Moscow, and they had captured another 348,000 Soviet soldiers, killed tens of thousands more, and accounted for three thousand tanks captured or destroyed. Small wonder that they failed to recognize any weaknesses in their position.

Army Group South faced a similar mix of confused orders and Soviet resistance in its efforts to take the western Ukraine, and also suffered from having gotten off to a slower start than its northern neighbors. At the end of June the army group held a line running roughly from north of Chelm on the Polish border southeast to a point east of Rovno, then southwest through Strij to the Hungarian border (see map 2). Kiev lay nearly 180 miles farther east, and indications were that the Soviets were reoccupying an old line of fortifications, the so-called Stalin Line, in the area of Novograd-Volynskiy. As elsewhere, the Wehrmacht found itself stronger than its opponent at any number of points, but still too weak to do everything it wanted, or needed, to do. The army group's main task, to surround and destroy all Soviet forces west of the Dnieper, looked less and less feasible; Soviet resistance was tougher than expected, and von Rundstedt was having to go through his available resources too quickly for the army group to advance through to Kiev and down the Dnieper. A closer encirclement, with a turn southeast by Armored Group 1 short of Kiev to meet up with Eleventh Army around Vinnitsa, seemed more realistic – but still the temptation to try for Kiev was almost irresistible, since its capture would provide a springboard for further operations. And so began a series of debates over the proper course to take, and a series of changes of course in the middle of the campaign, the end result being another imperfect victory.

Following a brief pause to reinforce their spearheads, von

Rundstedt's forces advanced again on 2 July. Armored Group 1 under von Kleist, along with most of von Reichenau's Sixth Army, moved east, breaking through the Stalin Line on the fifth, taking Berdichev on the seventh, and reaching Zhitomir on the ninth. Part of Sixth Army, along with von Stülpnagel's Seventeenth Army, also attacked southeast toward Ternopol, with support from Hungarian forces advancing northeast out of that country on their right. Eleventh Army moved deeper into Soviet territory from Romania, reaching the Dniester near Mogilev-Podolskij. But although some forces advanced over one hundred miles in less than a week, problems remained. Most seriously, on the northern flank Soviet forces had been attacking constantly out of the Pripet Marshes, disrupting Sixth Army's advance and severing supply lines. Both Sixth Army and Army Group Center had sent forces into the Pripet, but the Soviets had avoided those attacks and reappeared to hit the Germans at other points. The Soviets also kept up a constant series of attacks against the armored group's spearhead and against Eleventh Army in the south. And finally, heavy summer rains added to the Germans' difficulties.

After the fall of Zhitomir, the question of how to proceed became even more pressing, and there was simply no clear answer. The entire chain of command, from the different army headquarters up to Hitler himself, went back and forth over the various options, but the fact remained that the army group simply did not have the forces to deal with the Soviets in the Pripet, take Kiev, and execute an encirclement near Vinnitsa all at the same time. After several days of debate, during which Soviet attacks continued and the Germans attempted to replenish their forces, von Kleist's group turned southeast on 14 July, leaving Sixth Army in the north to deal with the Soviets in the Pripet and to hold in front of Kiev. By early August the armored forces had advanced as far as Kirovograd and Pervomaysk, and had encircled about twenty Soviet divisions in the area east of Uman, well south of Vinnitsa. The Germans captured a further 103,000 Soviet soldiers and large quantities of equipment in that encirclement. They had not, however, been able to establish a bridgehead on the east side of the Dnieper, nor had they destroyed the Soviet forces to the west of that river.

By the beginning of August, the Wehrmacht had chalked up some impressive gains. It had advanced hundreds of miles, and now appeared poised to take Leningrad, Moscow, and Kiev. Six weeks of battles had gutted most of the Red Army's best formations; the Soviets had lost thousands of tanks, guns, and aircraft, as well as hundreds of thousands of men. The Germans believed, with some justification, that they had their opponents on the ropes. Surely the Soviets could not have any great reserves of military power left. One more good push ought to seal the USSR's fate. On 23 July Halder declared to Hitler that the army would be in Leningrad and Moscow in another month, on the Volga River at the beginning of October, and a month after that in Baku and Batum in the Caucasus oil fields.

A careful examination of the situation reveals that Halder should not have been so sanguine. True, the Wehrmacht had demonstrated its superiority over the Red Army, but there were signs that all was not going smoothly. Germany's armies were having difficulty achieving their goals, even against a weak enemy. Where they could concentrate, they advanced without too much trouble, but they could not concentrate everywhere, and there were places – south of Leningrad, on the borders of the Pripet Marshes, and at Kiev, for example – where their strength proved inadequate. Moreover, the logistical situation was worrisome, or should have been, if the top generals had been paying attention. The army headquarters were already howling about supply shortages. Expenditures of fuel and ammunition were higher than expected. The main roads on the Wehrmacht's maps had proved to be dirt tracks in many cases; when vehicles were not choking on dust, they were stuck in mud. Road conditions and enemy action reduced the crucial transport units' vehicle strength by 25 to 30 per cent in the first month alone. The conversion of the Russian railroads to the German gauge was behind schedule as well, often

because the conversion crews found bypassed Soviet troops block-
ing the railway rights-of-way. Captured food supplies and transport
never reached expected quantities, and the coal and gasoline that fell
into German hands proved next to useless because of its poor quality.
Aerial resupply of some units proved necessary to overcome critical
shortages of fuel and ammunition. And casualties were high, as well;
as of 3 August, that is, six weeks into the campaign, Halder recorded
total losses numbering 179,500. Given that there were only three
hundred thousand replacements available, the Wehrmacht could not
continue to suffer such losses for much longer without losing fighting strength. The Germans were still depending upon a collapse of
the Soviet military and political systems. Without that collapse, their
problems would soon start to become acute – but in the rear areas,
meanwhile, the Germans were implementing policies that were
already beginning to strengthen Soviet resolve.

The War Behind the Lines Begins

Two major themes dominate an examination of German policies and
practices behind the lines. The first is a convergence of practical and
ideological considerations on the part of the occupiers. On the practical side, the military had an interest in securing the rear areas, both in
order to protect its supply lines and so that it would have a free hand in
exploiting the local economy. Any resistance on the part of partisans or
the local population would jeopardize both of those goals. In addition,
Nazi Party officials wanted to eliminate political and racial enemies, in
part to ensure German domination of the captured territories and in
part because they believed that the destruction of 'Jewish Bolshevism'
was an ideological goal in and of itself. To some extent these considerations overlapped; many members of the military accepted Nazi
ideology to one degree or another, while many Nazis also perceived
the 'practical' side of their actions for the military campaign.

The other major theme concerns a tension that existed between opposing German policy trends. On one side was that combination of practical and ideological goals just described, together with a belief in the power of brutality. Those factors encouraged the escalation of violence. On the other side was a desire to maintain military discipline and the perceived need to win over the populace, the former for the sake of combat effectiveness and the latter in order to eliminate the partisan threat and deprive the Red Army of a motive to keep fighting. In the end the first set of tendencies won out, in part because of their inherent power within German military and civilian institutions, and in part because, especially in this period, the Germans believed they could win the military campaign easily, and so did not see any need to moderate their policies toward noncombatants.

As one might guess from the range of criminal orders that the Germans issued in the weeks before the campaign began, the crimes that took place behind the front took the form of a complex stew, in which individual parts are difficult to separate from one another. Victim groups overlapped. The Germans often treated bypassed Soviet units as partisans, as they did some civilians. Many of those Soviet soldiers, partisans, and civilians were also Jews and Communists, while the majority were not. German policies sometimes lumped all these identities together and sometimes treated them separately – and those policies, in turn, often shaped the victims' own allegiances and acts. One must enter into any examination of German actions and their effects with this complexity firmly in mind. For the sake of clarity, we will examine different elements of German criminality separately, but the reality was that they all bled into one another.

The Treatment of Prisoners of War

From the very start of the campaign, the Wehrmacht began to capture Soviet soldiers, and the treatment it meted out to them was even more brutal than the plans had called for. That brutality began when Red Army soldiers surrendered, or attempted to. Although firm numbers are impossible to calculate, Wehrmacht troops shot many Soviet soldiers as they tried to give themselves up, and executed others, sometimes in groups, after they had surrendered. In part these acts grew out of the bloodlust that often governs men in battle, and on that level the killing was very much a two-way street: the Soviets were shooting German captives as well, in a war whose viciousness soon exceeded that on any other European front. There was a fundamental difference in the two sides' policies, however. The senior Nazi and Wehrmacht leaders had encouraged the expectation, before the campaign ever opened, that brutality would be the norm. Moreover, orders soon came from headquarters at many different levels, to the effect that no prisoners should be taken, or that groups of them were to be shot in retaliation for Soviet offenses. Some of the higher commanders, such as von Brauchitsch and von Kluge, countermanded such orders, on the basis that they would damage discipline and strengthen Russian resistance, but the practice continued and gradually expanded. Females in the Red Army were special targets. On June 29 von Kluge issued an order that all women in uniform were to be shot. The OKH countermanded the order, but soldiers at the front, along with their division headquarters, paid little attention.

Some of the front-line shootings came about as a direct result of the Commissar Order. In the Nuremberg trials and in their memoirs, senior field commanders such as Guderian denied that they had implemented the order, but their unit reports show otherwise; in fact, only one division indicated noncompliance. Many units, to the contrary, reported explicitly that they had carried out their instructions to the letter. The Wehrmacht Propaganda Office – part of the OKW – exhorted the troops to strike down the 'Jewish commissars,' on the theory that only they were keeping Soviet soldiers in the fight. While we have no firm numbers, the indications are that hundreds of Red Army political officers lost their lives before they ever saw the inside of a prisoner compound.

For those Red Army soldiers who managed to survive their first day or two in captivity, the ordeal was just beginning. The overall numbers were staggering. By 11 July, the Wehrmacht had captured more than 360,000 prisoners. By 5 August the number had risen to more than 774,000. One of the German army's first concerns was to control those masses of men, and to that end it looked to the Commissar Order as a mechanism and a model. On 10 July General Eugen Müller, von Brauchitsch's special assistant, spread the word in the commander in chief's name that commissars were thought to be removing their insignia and slipping into the POW compounds, which needed to be thoroughly searched. On 24 July General Wagner ordered that 'politically intolerable and suspicious elements, commissars, and agitators' be identified in the camps immediately and that camp commandants deal with them in accordance with the 'special directives,' that is, shoot them.[7] He expressly excluded the use of Security Police and SD units. Reports indicate that many camp commandants in the OKH zone carried out Wagner's instructions, although at least one of them disobeyed him and turned his prisoners over to the Security Police.

In the OKW zone, the military made full use of *Einsatzgruppen* units. Reinecke and Heydrich each worked out new orders, which they released on 17 July. Heydrich's order, 'Guidelines for the Cleansing of Prison Camps in Which Russians Are Housed,' called for the *Einsatzgruppen* to select and liquidate broad but precisely defined groups of prisoners in the OKW zone in East Prussia and the General Government. Those groups included all Communist Party and state functionaries, commissars, economic leaders, intelligentsia, and Jews. Shootings were to take place out of sight of the camps. The order from the OKW's POW Branch, on the other hand, enjoined camp commandants and other military authorities to cooperate with the *Einsatzgruppen* by, among other things, dividing the prisoners into groups according to their military status, political reliability, and ethnicity. The chief of the Gestapo, Heinrich Müller, followed up with his own order on 21 July, by which he sent his own detachments to camps in individual parts of the Reich, East Prussia, and the General Government. The German leaders were concerned that hard-core Communists not enter the Reich proper, where their poisonous ideas could damage morale – as they supposedly had in the First World War. Thus began a steady process of selection and murder that went on for the rest of the war.

The remainder of the prisoners did not face the prospect of summary execution for their politics or their race, but their chances were not much better in the long run. The treatment they received, in terms of food, housing, medical care, transport, and working conditions, although it did not kill them immediately, doomed almost all of them. The army put many of them to work; the rest faced a long journey through stages of the camp system until they finally arrived in camps in the OKW zone. That journey took place mostly on foot. The original plan had been to transport the prisoners on empty supply trucks returning from the front, so that long foot columns would not interfere with road traffic, but transport unit commanders usually refused to carry the prisoners, out of fear that their trucks would become infested with lice. On 31 July Wagner's office gave in and ordered that the prisoners be marched to their destinations. As the front advanced, the distances that the prisoners had to cover increased, until some of them were walking hundreds of miles over the course of weeks. On the way, no unit felt responsible for the prisoners, and their treatment suffered accordingly.

At the various stages in their journey, the prisoners spent time in the camps that the Wehrmacht had prepared for them. At this early stage of the campaign, when the Germans still believed that they would win easily, their plan was to keep the vast majority of the POWs in the zone of operations and the rest in the General Government and East Prussia, although a significant number did make it all the way back to Germany proper. The camps into which the prisoners flooded were minimal; the Germans often made the prisoners develop the sites themselves, and in most cases there was no provision for anything other than a wire enclosure and guard towers. The camps were not to receive prefabricated barracks; any shelter would be of the most primitive sort. In practice, prisoners slept on the bare ground or in holes, with nothing but their coats for shelter. This was the case even in the Reich, where material shortages were not an issue. Medical care was nonexistent; wounded prisoners were often simply shot, or segregated and allowed to die of their injuries.

Food was lacking as well. The OKH issued one general set of guidelines before the campaign, which stated that Soviet prisoners were to receive the smallest possible share of food. Beyond that, the local headquarters were free to use their own judgment, and so ration levels varied widely, but none of them was adequate. In Army Group Center, the ration was seven hundred calories per day, a starvation ration even for those who were not working. In other places the rations went as high as 1,300 calories for working prisoners and 2,035 calories for those on foot marches. The higher of those calorie levels came closer to adequacy, but in any case the figures were notional; they did not reflect what the prisoners actually received. Organizational problems combined with a straightforward lack of concern to deprive the prisoners of even the meager rations to which their captors thought them entitled. From an early point, various agencies complained that prisoners could not work because they were too weak from hunger.

The Wehrmacht's orders regarding the treatment of the POWs by their guards had always emphasized harshness. On 25 July Eugen Müller issued an order on von Brauchitsch's behalf that went still farther. Concerning prisoners of war, it said:

> The prisoner of war who is obedient and willing to work is to be treated decently. Anyone who acts against this regulation is to be punished in accordance with his offense.

> *It is in keeping with the standing and dignity of the German army that every German soldier preserve the distance and the attitude toward Russian prisoners of war that takes into account the fierceness and the inhuman brutality of the*

Russians in combat. Any leniency or even an attempt to curry favor is to be punished most harshly. The feeling of pride and superiority must remain recognizable at all times.[8]

The order further commanded the guards to use their weapons immediately at the first sign of insubordination or rebellion on the part of their charges. Escaping prisoners were to be shot without warning. Any hesitation, Müller insisted, represented a danger. Escaped Soviet prisoners whom the Germans recaptured were often shot – somewhat less often in the OKH zone, but almost always in the OKW zone.

The Treatment of Enemy Civilians and the Antipartisan Campaign

The Wehrmacht's senior leaders never issued any written guidelines for their administration of the occupied territories, beyond the rather general orders of 13 March and 3 April, which did little more than advise German soldiers to be forceful and absolve them of any crimes in advance. The army believed that its role as an occupying force in Russia would be brief, that it would defeat the Soviet government and conquer the territory, after which the political authorities would take over. There was no plan for a military administration, and there were not enough security forces to go around, if any kind of widespread resistance developed. The initial plan was that the army's security divisions would control the main transportation arteries, while the *Einsatzgruppen* and police units pacified the countryside. The army's leadership emphasized, above all, that its units establish order in the rear areas and exploit the conquered regions in order to relieve the burden on the supply system. Commanders at the army and army group levels therefore implemented whatever policies they saw fit. Significant discrepancies existed from one area to another, and often between different levels of command.

One should note that when the army first entered Soviet territory, the reception it received from local inhabitants was often enthusiastic. The Baltic states had only recently lost their independence to Stalin, and Belorussia and the Ukraine had long nursed a wish to break away from the USSR. After early July, when the Soviets began implementing a scorched-earth campaign, even more local civilians were ready to rid themselves of the Soviet regime. Many of them saw the advancing German troops as liberators. Wehrmacht soldiers often received flowers and traditional welcome gifts of bread and salt, as well as the admiration of local ladies. The Wehrmacht's first declarations tended to encourage such friendliness. Protection would be available to anyone who worked hard and obeyed instructions, they said. German commanders also set up local authorities, drawing upon men whom the Security Police and SD had cleared, and used them to maintain order, register the population, and issue identification papers. Initial announcements also made clear that the open hand could become a fist: various acts, including espionage, sabotage, guerrilla activity, or the possession of weapons, radios, or Communist literature, were punishable by death. These were common practices, however, covered by the usages of war. Few among the civilian population imagined that the authorities in Berlin could possibly be worse than those in Moscow.

If those people had been aware of German food policy, their fears would have been greater. Certainly there was no hint that the 'hunger plan' might be tempered by kindness as the campaign unfolded. Two days after the invasion started, State Secretary Backe argued that, in addition to the food that the army would need in order to feed itself, the occupation authorities would need to ship six hundred thousand tons of grain back to Germany, because of the shortfall that the loss of trade with the Soviet Union had created. Backe's decision did not disturb the army much. True, some conflicts were already arising with the Economic Staff East, which wanted to take a greater share of food than the army wanted to release. At this stage the army was feeding itself fairly well, however, and many planners believed that a quick end to the campaign and the subsequent reduction in army strength would eliminate any difficulties. On July 31 Backe was able to report that, over and above what the Wehrmacht had received, the Reich had procured around five hundred thousand tons of grain and one hundred thousand tons of meat. The prospects for the future were less positive, since the advancing armies had not found the large stocks of surplus food that the Soviets were thought to have in reserve. Food for the local population, and especially for the cities, would thus be in short supply; their demands would always take second place. On 8 July Hitler even remarked to Halder that he intended to level Moscow and Leningrad, to make them uninhabitable, so that there would be no need to feed their populations through the winter; such was the Nazi leadership's determination that Germans not suffer. So far there was little serious hunger among the conquered peoples of the east, but that situation could not last long.

Along with food, Germany also needed labor, and the occupying authorities began procuring it as soon as the campaign opened. The first targets were Polish, Lithuanian, and Belorussian farm laborers from the Baltic states. General Thomas authorized recruiting efforts on 3 July, and the first recruiting teams entered Lithuania about ten days later. By mid-August they had recruited fifteen thousand people for labor in East Prussia. At this early stage the program was neither as widespread nor as brutal as it would become eventually. There was as yet no move to recruit industrial workers, and the laborers in question were lured with false promises rather than driven at the point of a bayonet. Only with changes in the Germans' military fortunes at the end of the year would policies become more radical.

In the shorter term, Soviet civilians suffered more immediately from the Germans' fundamental biases and their efforts to establish military and political control. Wehrmacht commanders displayed some degree of sympathy for the sufferings of the locals under Stalinism, but they generally regarded enemy civilians as dirty, dishonest, racially inferior, and probably hostile. The Germans wanted the locals' cooperation, but only insofar as it was available without sacrifice on the part of the occupiers, and most of the time the latter allowed their arrogance and distrust to win out over any desire to establish friendly relations. The events around Minsk offer an example of Wehrmacht practice, albeit an extreme one. At the end of June the army drove forty thousand of the city's men between the ages of eighteen and fifty into a vast internment camp, where they joined more than one hundred thousand prisoners of war. The camp was so small that the prisoners could not move; they went without food for days at a stretch and had to relieve themselves where they stood. On 7 July von Kluge ordered the Secret Field Police and *Einsatzgruppe* B to comb through the camp in search of suspicious elements – despite Wagner's instructions not to involve the SS – and they murdered approximately two hundred people every day for the next two months. After the war Soviet authorities found about ten thousand bodies in nearby mass graves.

The dominant driving force behind such actions was the belief that the only way to deter or eliminate resistance to German occupation was to employ a maximum of brutality. The practice gained additional impetus from the fact that the Germans had so few forces with which to control their new conquests; in their eyes, they could not afford to be lenient. A partisan war was already in the offing. On 3 July Stalin issued the first of many calls for armed resistance against the invaders. On 14 July the Germans captured a Soviet report on the organization of the partisan campaign, including information on units, missions, tactics, and weapons. Hitler was not slow to act on such news. 'This partisan war has its advantages, as well,' he told several of his senior leaders during a discussion of occupation policy. 'It gives us the opportunity to stamp out everything that stands against us.' The best way to pacify such a large area, he insisted, is to 'shoot dead anyone who even looks at us askance.'[9] Wilhelm Keitel, chief of the Armed Forces High Command (OKW), echoed the sentiment and called for collective reprisals in response to any act of resistance. Soon the military authorities were translating the leaders' intentions into orders. On 18 July Eugen Müller issued a decree stating that any armed formations found behind the German front, whether they identified themselves as soldiers, former soldiers, or civilians, were to be treated as guerrillas, that is, shot, along with any civilians who lent them aid. As a result, German units shot thousands of Soviet stragglers out of hand. On 23 July the OKW decreed that it would not base the antipartisan campaign on the punishment of the guilty, but rather would concentrate on 'striking such terror into the population that it loses all will to resist.'[10] The 25 July order from von Brauchitsch and Müller, mentioned earlier, also addressed the antipartisan war. It opened by deploring the fact that 'the necessary severity of action is not being exercised everywhere.' 'The Russian,' it said, 'has always been used to hard, merciless action on the part of the authorities.'[11] It repeated the same arguments that had appeared so often before, about the Soviets' perfidity and the need for harsh measures in order to combat it. Any leniency would be taken as a sign of weakness and would endanger the troops in the long run, it said, and called for collective measures in any case of passive resistance, or when the guilty could not be identified.

If there was a bright side to that order, it was the acknowledgement that some significant portion of German soldiers were proving unwilling to toe the Nazi line. That being said, however, efforts at the more senior levels to moderate German occupation policies were partial at best, and ultimately all but meaningless. There were, notably, officers within the OKH and lower levels of the army who believed that more lenient policies would be more productive. They remarked on the enthusiastic reception that the Wehrmacht received in some areas, as well as on the fact that acts of sabotage were still uncommon. The solution they proposed, however, reveals the limits of their leniency. On 6 July, for example, General Hoepner decreed that in order to ensure proper treatment for the local population, his troops were to blame acts of sabotage on 'individual Communist elements, above all Jews.'[12] Other headquarters at army, corps, and division level issued similar orders, emphasizing that not all local elements were hostile and that acts of resistance should be blamed on

Russians, Communists, and Jews. On 12 July the OKH confirmed the policy, and reports from the field reveal efforts to follow it by shooting hostages or destroying homes only within the Russian and Jewish communities. This was no fundamental change in the brutality of the German occupation policy, but only a nod toward its selective implementation. In any case, the harshness of the whole regime soon made such selectivity all but moot.

As for the effectiveness of German policies, even at this stage they seldom did any good, and in many cases they did harm. The food requisitions, abuse of POWs, forced labor drafts, and mass imprisonments and executions would have created resentment in any case, but their effects went deeper, because of the contrast with earlier experiences of German occupation. Older inhabitants of the east remembered the last time German armies had occupied their land and captured their soldiers, in the First World War, and they had passed that memory on to the younger generations. At that time the Germans had been arrogant, but mostly correct in their behavior; they had been interested in reforming and improving the local population, not enslaving and exterminating it. Now the locals saw an entirely different side of the Germans, a seemingly inhuman side, and it came as a profound shock. They reacted by siding more and more with the emerging partisan movement and thus increasing the Germans' security problems. By the end of July six German divisions were engaged in antipartisan warfare in the east, in addition to the security forces, local auxiliaries, and units of Germany's allies.

Initial Measures against the Jews

When Hitler commented that the emerging partisan war offered an opportunity to stamp out anything that stood in the way of German domination, he was not only referring to the campaign against armed resistance groups. The conflation of Jews and Bolsheviks with one another and with sources of resistance was at the center of his thinking and that of his principal subordinates. They saw the elimination of the Jews as a goal in and of itself, but also as a key to destroying the Soviet state and exerting control in the conquered lands. Additionally, an exterminationist policy offered a quick way to save quantities of food by eliminating so-called useless mouths. Debate continues among historians to this day over the point at which Hitler decided to eliminate the Jews of the Soviet Union physically, whether before or during the campaign, but the fact of the decision is plain. The Jews would be the first targets for abuse, forced labor, and, ultimately, extermination.

The execution of policies against the Jews was, first and foremost, the province of the SS *Einsatzgruppen*, along with police and Waffen-SS units. These groups had received authorization from the army's leaders to carry out their special missions in the army and army group rear areas, to include securing important individuals such as saboteurs, terrorists, and leading émigrés. No written orders said anything about Jews before the campaign opened, but the evidence indicates that at some point in the weeks preceding the invasion, Heydrich informed the commanders of the *Einsatzgruppen* orally as to the true nature of their mission, part of which was to kill anyone who constituted a threat to the regime, including Jews. Then, ten days after the campaign began, Heydrich instructed the Higher SS and Police Leaders, who oversaw the *Einsatzgruppen* and other police units, to execute all Communist Party functionaries, plus 'Jews in Party and state positions, and other radical elements (saboteurs, propagandists, snipers, assassins, agitators, etc.).'[13] Actually, from the very start of the campaign, the *Einsatzgruppen* operated well outside the limits that their orders – or at least the written ones – had set. For one thing, they did not only perform their tasks in the rear areas; by mid-July their detachments were following in the wake of the army's foremost troops, in order to catch their victims before they had a chance to escape. And despite Heydrich's written instructions that targeted 'Jews in Party and state positions,' the killings were much more widespread from the start.

The *Einsatzgruppen* used a couple of different tactics in their war on the Jews, one of which was to trigger or intensify pogroms – massacres – by local inhabitants against their Jewish neighbors, preferably without leaving any evidence of German involvement. This tactic had two purposes: first, to take some of the workload off the *Einsatzgruppen* themselves, and, second, to place a major part of the responsibility for the killings on the locals and simultaneously 'prove' how unpopular the Jews were. In some areas, such as the Baltic states, these efforts were somewhat successful, in that pogroms did indeed take place, usually after a certain amount of instigation on the part of the Germans. In Kaunas, for example, a detachment of *Einsatzgruppe* A encouraged Lithuanian partisans (whom the Germans had discovered fighting Red Army troops as they entered the city) to attack Jews. The Lithuanians killed over 3,800 Jews in Kaunas and another 1,200 in other towns between 24 and 29 June. Another four hundred died in a pogrom in Riga after the *Einsatzgruppe* reached that city. Farther south, *Einsatzgruppe* C was able to start some pogroms in areas of Galicia where Poles and Ukrainians dominated. All told, thousands of Jews and others fell victim to German-inspired pogroms. On the whole, however, the Germans were disappointed with many local citizens' unwillingness to attack their Jewish neighbors, and the victim count remained lower than the instigators had hoped.

The other, and predominating, tactic was to simply enter a town, round up the intended victims, take them to a more-or-less remote area nearby, and shoot them. In this first period of the conflict these so-called actions targeted mostly people whom the Germans considered a threat, especially Bolsheviks, members of the Jewish intelligentsia, and Jewish men of military age. As the scale of the task became plainer, the Germans augmented their forces. In mid-July, eleven Order Police battalions and other SS units deployed to the east on 'cleansing operations,' and the Germans also recruited thousands of local auxiliaries from the same sorts of groups that had carried out the massacre in Kaunas. Together with the *Einsatzgruppen*, in these first six weeks of the war they killed tens of thousands of Jews, along with Soviet officials, Communist sympathizers, criminals, the handicapped, prisoners of war, stragglers, hostages, and anyone who offered any resistance to German rule. In many cases the actual nature of the victims remains in doubt, as when units reported liquidating '1,542 persons (predominantly Jews)' or '500 Jews, among them saboteurs'; the perpetrators developed a thoroughly euphemistic system for describing the killings and their victims.[14]

Where was the army in all this? To a greater or lesser extent depending on the circumstances, its attitude, at least in the upper echelons, varied between nervous resignation and enthusiastic support. In any case there was usually no lack of cooperation with the *Einsatzgruppen* and the other killing squads. Dr. Walther Stahlecker, head of *Einsatzgruppe* A, reported on 4 July that he was receiving excellent cooperation from Eighteenth Army headquarters, and similar reports were the norm. The cooperation took several forms. The army provided the murder squads with their supplies, ammunition, transport, and housing, without which they could hardly have carried out their missions. During the killings themselves, the army usually remained 'neutral' at best, as in the case of Kaunas, when hundreds of Wehrmacht soldiers and officers watched as the slaughter took place; those who objected were told not to intervene. At other times the army took a more active role. Army units, such as security divisions under the command of the army group rear area headquarters, sometimes identified, segregated, and guarded the victims; at other times they cordoned off the areas where shootings occurred. In Lvov, the local commander went so far as to help instigate a pogrom himself. When army units entered the city early on 30 June, they discovered the corpses of four thousand prisoners whom the Soviet secret police, the NKVD, had killed. By noon posters had gone up at the local army headquarters, blaming the Jews for the killings, and soon Ukrainian nationalists, including a battalion under German command and in German uniform, launched an orgy of rape, pillage, beatings, and murder against the Jewish community that lasted until the next day. Later the army used pictures of the NKVD murders to further indoctrinate its troops against 'Jewish Bolshevism.' Not until

1 July did elements of *Einsatzgruppe* C arrive to put the killings on a more orderly basis. (In other instances army officers stepped in to stop pogroms, in order to preserve military discipline and keep riots from getting out of hand, but such cases were not the norm.)

The army tried to justify its cooperation in part by maintaining, however weakly, that a link existed between Jews and partisans. That was the basis upon which commanders controlled the murder squads and directed them to particular targets, or aided in the squads' operations; the distinctions were just blurred enough to provide a thin facade of correctness, at least as far as the army was concerned. During the capture of Daugavpils, for example, the local corps headquarters justified actions against the Jews on the grounds that they were guilty of sabotage against the troops 'directly or indirectly.'[15] Sometimes such justifications were even enough to spur direct involvement in the killings. On 2 July an infantry platoon assisted in the shooting of 1,160 Jews in reprisal for the killing of ten Wehrmacht soldiers. In another instance, troops in Zloczow shot several hundred Jews in retaliation for the killing of Ukrainians by the Soviets. SS units also took part in the 'antipartisan' war. On 19 July, Himmler put the 2nd SS Cavalry Brigade at the disposal of Higher SS and Police Leader Erich von dem Bach-Zelewski, purportedly to fight partisans in the Pripet Marshes. At the end of the month he issued detailed guidelines for the unit's use: in areas in which the population was hostile, racially inferior, or criminal, the men were to be shot, the women and children deported, and the villages razed. Up until 12 August, the brigade shot 13,788 people whom they termed looters, with a loss of two dead and fifteen wounded. Such numbers hardly spoke of battles with partisans, but that did not appear to matter, either to the SS or to the army headquarters with which they coordinated their operations.

In some areas the army also played a leading role in setting up ghettos in which to segregate and control the Jews. Ghettoization was a local matter at this point in the war; the central authorities in Berlin did not involve themselves in such decisions. Local conditions shaped policy, especially the lack of housing in cities such as Minsk, Smolensk, and Vitebsk, where military operations had destroyed thousands of homes. Squeezing the Jews into restricted quarters would free up space for other ethnic groups whom the Germans wanted to court. Controlling the Jews in this way would also save food, since their rations could be cut to nearly nothing, and would help the occupying authority to control the labor market, again providing opportunities for other groups. And so the army set up a ghetto in Minsk, for example, with a decree of 19 July that ordered all the Jews into a defined area of the city within five days. In this case *Einsatzgruppe* B played a purely advisory role. In other places the SS organized ghettos, and in still others, no ghetto ever came into being; there was no consistency across the occupied territories, except that when the time came to clear the ghettos and kill the inhabitants; that was the job of the SS and police.

Within the army itself, the effects of its cooperation with the SS were insidious. There were, all along, a few army commanders who attempted to prevent their troops from taking part in, or even observing, the killing actions. The commanders' concern, though, just as had been true of von Brauchitsch during the planning process, and before that in connection with SS activities in Poland, was usually with troop discipline, rather than with fundamental moral questions. The officer corps did not want their troops running amok. That, however, is exactly what happened in far too many cases. Most significantly, the army's rationale for the killings – that they were part of the antipartisan campaign – broke down as soon as units began shooting young children. As the facade became increasingly transparent, troop discipline deteriorated.

The beginning of August 1941 marked a moment of immense confidence in the German camp. The military campaign seemed to be going according to plan; the armies had achieved most of their initial objectives, and the Red Army appeared to be on its last legs. The goal of pacifying and exploiting the rear areas also seemed to be well in hand. Food and other resources were already flowing to the Reich, political enemies were being eliminated, and the partisan threat would surely prove ephemeral once the army had finished with the main Soviet forces and the Stalinist government was no more. That their situation might not be so positive as it seemed was not a thought that occurred to the Wehrmacht's leaders. In the high Russian summer, everything seemed possible.

4

The Second Phase: Expanding Conquests and Genocide, August to October

A real sense of possibility permeated the German leadership's upper echelons at the beginning of August. Ultimate victory seemed certain. The Wehrmacht had defeated the best units that the Red Army could throw against it, and German forces threatened three of the USSR's greatest cities: Leningrad, Moscow, and Kiev. The Soviets had seldom been able to stand for long against the Germans at any point where the latter chose to concentrate their efforts. Materially, tactically, and operationally, the Wehrmacht simply outclassed its opponent. At the same time, though, nagging doubts were emerging, like the buzzing of a fly that that the generals kept trying to brush away. Most important, the Red Army was proving much stronger, or at least much larger, than the German commanders had expected. According to their original concept, by the time they reached the Dvina and the Dnieper they expected to have destroyed the Soviet military, and they supposed the rest of the campaign would be easy. Events were not working out that way. True, the Red Army could not stop the Germans where the latter were strong – but the Wehrmacht could not be strong everywhere, and somehow the Soviets kept fighting. The Germans had to find a way to finish them, and quickly. In the coming weeks the German leaders would debate bitterly among themselves, then launch another brilliant stroke, but find that the knockout still eluded them. Meanwhile, as their victories gained them more and more territory, their policies toward their captive enemies and the native population would become even more radical.

Operations in August: Army Group North

In the last week of July, Army Group North's front line described a broad arc, from the northeastern corner of the Gulf of Riga to Lake Peipus, up to Narva, then southeast to the shore of Lake Ilmen and south to a point just west of Velikie Luki and the border with Army Group Center (see map 1). The Soviets were still holding on to the northwestern portion of Estonia around Tallinn as well as territory south of Leningrad, and they threatened the army group along that long southern flank as well. Von Leeb had shifted most of Hoepner's Armored Group 4 to the area south and east of Narva, where it could drive on Leningrad along terrain that was at least moderately well suited for tanks, thickly forested though it was. The main problem for von Leeb was that he did not possess enough strength to take Leningrad – a top priority for Hitler – while protecting his southern flank at the same time. He wanted to pull Hoth's Armored Group 3 out of Army Group Center and into his battle by sending it east of Lake Ilmen and then north to cut off Leningrad's supply lines, but Halder was dead set against such an option; he wanted to save Armored Group 3 for a drive on Moscow. Halder suggested that von Leeb use his own armored forces farther east, to thrust from either side of Lake Ilmen toward Lake Ladoga, but this idea ignored (not for the first time) the fact that tanks would bog down in the swamps that covered the area. In early August the two men compromised; von Leeb would indeed attack northeastward via Novgorod toward Lake Ladoga, but mostly with infantry from Sixteenth Army; Armored Group 4 would continue its attack from the area east of

Narva (see map 3). Von Leeb thought he was going to get support from Armored Group 3, but Halder succeeded in preventing that deployment.

Armored Group 4's attack kicked off on 8 August, but its initial progress was minimal. While the Germans had been debating, regrouping, and resupplying, the Soviets had been building up their defenses. Hoepner's tanks suffered heavy losses, and not until August 10, when Sixteenth Army's attack opened, did the Soviet front begin to crumble, and then only slowly. Then, on 13 August, von Leeb's fears for his southern front became reality as the Soviets attacked there. Von Leeb had warned the OKH that his forces along that line – a few divisions from Sixteenth Army – were too weak; now he doubted that the front could hold without reinforcements, which he could only send if he stopped the attack on Leningrad. In reaction to this new Soviet thrust, Hitler ordered that Army Group Center transfer two motorized corps from Armored Group 3 to von Leeb's command. Halder tried to insist that these corps go to the attack on Novgorod, again revealing his curious blindness to the terrain conditions there. Instead, von Leeb put the new units to work directly against the Soviet attack, and managed to stabilize the front. In the meantime the army group's offensive finally began to make some significant gains. The eastern prong passed Novgorod and reached Chudovo by 20 August, cutting the most direct rail link between Leningrad and Moscow. Farther west, Armored Group 4 took Krasnogvardeysk and cut the rail line supplying the Soviet forces at Luga. Narva fell on 17 August, and the Germans also advanced farther toward Tallinn.

On 29 August Army Group North's headquarters issued orders for the continuation of the campaign against Leningrad. Under this plan, the Germans would not try to take the city by storm, but rather cut it off from water, food, and energy supplies and so force its surrender. On 31 August von Leeb and his chief of staff were already thinking of the next stage: once the city was surrounded, they could withdraw some units to take part in the attack on Moscow. Von Leeb assumed that the Soviets would see the hopelessness of Leningrad's position and give it up without much of a battle; he drew that conclusion in part because intelligence reports noted that the Soviets were evacuating industrial facilities and some civilians. He was mistaken. The Soviets intended to fight for Russia's old capital.

Army Group South: To the Dnieper

By the first week of August, Army Group South held a growing bulge of territory, spreading from the southern fringes of the Pripet Marshes south of Korosten southeast to Kirovograd and then back southwest through Pervomaysk and Balta to the Dniester. Eleventh Army, with Germany's Romanian allies, held most of the area west of the Dniester. The remains of nine Soviet divisions were fighting out their last in the pocket east of Uman (see map 2). The army group still faced the difficulty that the front was increasing in breadth, while the available forces were steadily losing strength in an offensive that lacked a natural focus. Von Rundstedt's goals were ambitious: Kiev, Odessa, the Donets basin industrial zone, the Crimea, and beyond to the Caucasus and Stalingrad, all the while securing vast amounts of occupied territory and enormous fronts. Even if the Soviets had collapsed as the Germans had expected, merely occupying such a vast expanse would have been daunting. And the Soviets were not collapsing.

As of 21 July, the army group's plan had been to cross the Dnieper at Cherkassy, Dnepropetrovsk, or Zaporozhye and head straight for the Donets basin (see map 4). To that end von Rundstedt wanted to concentrate his forces in the great bend of the Dnieper. Hitler and Halder, however, were insisting that von Rundstedt drive south via Pervomaysk to reach the Black Sea as soon as possible, in order to cut off the Soviet forces that were holding out west of the Bug River. The Soviets added to the Germans' dilemma in the first week of August by attacking Sixth Army again from out of the Pripet and from the area around Kiev. Von Reichenau was concerned that he might not be able to hold on his northern flank; he wanted more help from Army Group Center to relieve the pressure. On 12 August he got it: Second Army and Armored Group 2 attacked southward from their positions near Rogachev and Roslavl toward the area between Gomel and Bryansk, in an effort to cut off the Soviet units in the Pripet (see map 5). Despite significant gains on that front, though, the pressure on Sixth Army did not ease. A few days before, Halder had been of the opinion that von Rundstedt's forces were sufficient for his mission; he believed that the encirclement at Uman and other operations had destroyed the Red Army's entire southern wing. Perhaps, he thought, the army group might even be able to transfer units to Army Group Center for the advance on Moscow. The continuing attacks against Sixth Army shattered that picture. Now von Rundstedt split Armored Group 1 and sent part of it to the northern front to help halt the Soviet attacks, while he told von Reichenau to stop his attack on Kiev. Preparations for further offensive operations would have to wait while the situation stabilized.

On 12 August von Brauchitsch issued a directive that focused von Rundstedt's effort toward the south and southeast. The army group's major task for the immediate future would be to clear all the territory west of the Dnieper and prepare for further advances southward and eastward toward the Crimea, Kharkov, and the Donets basin. Sixth Army was to abandon the drive on Kiev and instead attack north into the Pripet. At this point Halder was still expecting that operations west of the Dnieper would wipe out the last organized resistance in the south, and that advances beyond the river would be much easier. Soon, he hoped, he would be able to transfer more forces to Army Group Center – his constant theme. By 20 August von Rundstedt's armies did indeed control all the land west of the Dnieper, except for a pocket around the port of Odessa, and had taken some bridgeheads on the eastern side of the river as well. Sixth Army, however, remained tied down by attacks from the Pripet and Kiev. At this point the OKH began to think seriously about using von Bock's and von Rundstedt's army groups to eliminate the threat from the Pripet once and for all.

Moscow or the Ukraine?

While von Rundstedt's and von Leeb's forces were dealing with their own relatively local challenges, the debate between Hitler and his military advisors over the course of the campaign flared up again. Halder had never let go of his desire to take the Soviet capital, as is clear from his unceasing attempts to transfer forces to Army Group Center. He believed that the Soviets would throw all their reserves into the battle for Moscow and thus give the Wehrmacht the chance to destroy them utterly. Hitler, on the other hand, saw more value in gaining control of the Baltic by taking Leningrad, as well as in acquiring the Ukraine's economic assets. Both sides had let the matter rest as the Smolensk encirclement ran its course, but now, at the end of July, that battle was ending, Moscow lay a little over two hundred miles farther east, and a decision was unavoidable. There was certainly no sign that Hitler's views had changed since the last discussion of the subject. On 4 August, as the Smolensk pocket collapsed, he visited von Bock, to whom he explained his priorities again. Leningrad was the most important goal, he said, then the Donets basin and the rest of the Ukraine. Moscow was third on his list. He said the same thing to von Rundstedt two days later. Neither man could change the Führer's mind. While visiting Army Group South, Hitler also insisted that von Rundstedt and von Bock cooperate to eliminate the Soviet forces operating in the Pripet.

On 7 August Halder called on Jodl to enlist his aid in bringing Hitler around to the General Staff's point of view. He argued that all three of Hitler's objectives were important, but that army groups North and South were strong enough to take their objectives on their own. The Führer had to see the need to concentrate all available forces in the center – and to that end the two men decided that a small deception was in order. The next day Jodl presented Hitler with a situation report that showed most of the Soviets' forces arrayed in front of Moscow and understated the Red Army's strength elsewhere. He recommended an attack in the center against the Soviet capital in order to eliminate that concentration. Hitler apparently accepted his subordinate's assessment of the situation – but not his recommendations. On 12 August he issued Directive 34a, in which he ordered that the army take Moscow before winter set in. That statement appeared to be a victory for the generals; at least the Führer was now acknowledging Moscow's importance. The balance of the order must have been a disappointment, however, for it revealed that Hitler still wanted the army to capture the other objectives first, and he turned Halder's and Jodl's arguments on their heads by maintaining that since the Soviets were strong in front of Moscow, the Wehrmacht would have to strike where they were weak. He again insisted that von Rundstedt and von Bock cooperate to eliminate the Soviet forces in the Pripet; that von Rundstedt also take the Crimea, the Donets basin, and the area around Kharkov; and that von Leeb take Leningrad – all before the attack on Moscow could begin.

Halder was unhappy with the order, of course, but he still believed that he could launch the attack on Moscow in August, so long as the buildup and reorganization in Army Group Center could go forward without interference. The greatest threat to the plan appeared to be Soviet pressure against that army group's southern flank, but Second Army was preparing to eliminate that, as well as easing the pressure on Sixth Army, with its attack via Rogachev to Gomel. Halder's plans fell apart once again on 13 August, however, when the Red Army attacked Army Group North between Kholm and Staraya Russa, prompting Hitler to order parts of Armored Group 3 to reinforce von Leeb.

Halder, von Brauchitsch, and Jodl tried yet again on 18 August to change Hitler's mind. The OKW presented a new assessment, and von Brauchitsch produced a memorandum entitled 'Suggestion for the continuation of the operation of Army Group Center in connection with the operations of army groups South and North.' Both documents made essentially the same points as the army's leaders had made before: the Soviets had concentrated their forces in front of Moscow; the destruction of those forces would leave the Soviets without a coherent defense; and the northern and southern army groups could carry out their tasks alone. Von Brauchitsch proposed mobile thrusts from the area of Toropets via Rzhev and from the area of Bryansk via Kaluga, while the center would remain on the defensive for the most part. The two wings could turn inward either in front of or behind Moscow, depending on how the offensive developed. Von Brauchitsch stipulated that, in order for these attacks to go forward in time, the diversion of von Bock's forces to the north and south would have to cease.

The generals could have saved themselves the effort. An OKW memo of 20 August stated, 'The Führer is not in agreement with the commander-in-chief of the army's suggestion of 18 August for the continuation of operations. The problem is not Moscow and the strong enemy forces gathered there; it is much more urgent to eliminate the Russian industrial areas or to take them for our own use.'[1] In another memorandum of 21 August, and in a long 'study' dated 22 August, Hitler again explained, at great length, his strategic and operational considerations. He again insisted that Leningrad, the Donets basin, the Crimea, and the Soviet oil supplies in the Caucasus were the most important objectives. He also saw an operational opportunity developing. Kiev now sat at the western end of an enormous salient that was filled with Soviet units. Cut off that salient, destroy those forces, and the way would lie open to the more distant goals in the south. Moreover, such a move would also eliminate the southern threat to any advance on Moscow. That later advance, Hitler continued, would have to consist of a series of small encirclements, not the grand envelopment that Halder and von Brauchitsch had in mind. Practically speaking, these memorandums marked the end of the debate. Halder somehow held on to the hope that he could limit the use of Army Group Center's units and so get them back soon for the attack on Moscow, and his orders to Armored Group 2 departed from Hitler's wishes to some extent, with that goal in mind. The fact remained, however, that no attack on the Soviet capital could go forward until Hitler was satisfied with the progress to the north and south.

In a sense, one could say that the debate over this turn in the campaign has never ended. Some authors have claimed that Hitler let victory – in *Barbarossa* and even in the war – slip from his grasp when he turned his armies aside from Moscow. In truth, the debate almost certainly was and remains moot. For one thing, the Germans' logistical system was already experiencing serious problems. Repairs to the railroads had not kept pace with the advance, so the number of trains getting through to Army Group Center's rear area each day remained below the level the armies required for daily operations. The railheads, moreover, remained up to 450 miles behind the front; that fact, plus the horrendous condition of the roads, led to an increased breakdown rate among the transportation units, adding to the delays and shortages. All this meant that the Germans could scrape together enough supplies to send Guderian south against light opposition, but there was no way they could build up the reserves that von Bock's armies would have needed to make the distance to Moscow, even if Hitler had allowed them to. Even holding in place proved difficult for the next few weeks, as the Soviets made their strongest counterattacks yet against von Bock's forces in front of Smolensk, starting in mid-August. Then and later, the Soviets took great pride in their performance during this Battle of Smolensk, as they called it. For the first time, they actually drove the Germans back, retaking Yelna, which von Bock had wanted to keep as a springboard for later operations. But although the German troops there were still better equipped and trained than their opponents, von Bock could not get enough munitions to them to stave off the Soviet attacks, so at the beginning of September he had to abandon the town.

Supply problems aside – they never entered into the debates at the top in any case – by this time there were no options that would have guaranteed a German victory, even if the Wehrmacht had been able to advance to Moscow and surround it. Such an advance would have left a long southern flank open to attack, as well as lengthening the supply lines even further. More importantly, the Red Army was still showing no signs of collapse, as even the Germans were having to admit. On 6 August Jodl's deputy, Walter Warlimont, produced a memo entitled 'Brief strategic overview on the continuation of the war after the campaign in the east,' in which he said that the Wehrmacht would not be able to reach its operational goals – a line from the Caucasus oil region to the Volga and on to Archangel and Murmansk – in 1941, and so an open front would remain in existence. By the end of the month Hitler had also come around to that view. And on 11 August, a scant five weeks after he pronounced the Russian army defeated, Halder confided to his diary:

> The whole situation makes it increasingly plain that we have underestimated the Russian colossus, who consistently prepared for war with that utterly ruthless determination so characteristic of totalitarian states. . . . At the outset of the war, we reckoned with about 200 enemy divisions. Now we have already counted 360. Indeed these divisions are not armed and equipped according to our standards, and their tactical leadership is often poor. But they are there, and if we smash a dozen of them, the Russians simply put up another dozen.[2]

What was true for the Red Army was also true for the Soviet government. The Soviets were ready to defend Moscow tooth and nail, but they were also ready to evacuate it if need be. They were already preparing defenses to the east of the city, and the region around Gorkii, 250 miles beyond Moscow, offered good north-south railroad connections to support the defenders logistically. While one cannot absolutely rule out a political collapse if Moscow had fallen, it appears highly unlikely. Barring such a collapse, the fall of Moscow would not have won the campaign for Germany.

Encirclement in the Ukraine

In an odd way, the long debate within the German high command worked in the Wehrmacht's favor. Stalin believed, based on high-level intelligence, that the Germans would strike at Moscow via Bryansk, and Guderian's thrust southward from Smolensk seemed to support that view. In fact Stalin was correct – inasmuch as he understood the German generals' intentions. The problem was, of course, that the generals were not in charge, and at first Stalin had no way of knowing about Hitler's decision to attack into the Ukraine from the north. In order to counter the attack he expected on the capital, Stalin created a new headquarters for the Bryansk sector, but he oriented its forces along a north–south axis, leaving the area south of Guderian's forces relatively open. He then disbanded the headquarters that stood most directly in Guderian's path and placed its units under the Bryansk command. By that time Stalin was aware of the Germans' intentions, but he believed his forces could stop Armored Group 2 with counter-attacks, and so he refused to authorize a withdrawal from Kiev. While the Bryansk headquarters was in the middle of taking over its new units, which were weak from prolonged combat in any case, the Germans struck.

On 25 August, Armored Group 2 began its advance south-ward from the area just north of the Desna River (see map 5). The Soviets launched heavy counterattacks against both of the armored group's flanks, and at one point Guderian had to call for reinforcements, but the Soviets could not stop the tank units' progress. By 10 September the Germans had reached the town of Romny. In the meantime, Seventeenth Army seized crossings over the Dnieper at Kremenchug, in battles that lasted from 30 August to 2 September. On 4 September von Rundstedt ordered von Stülpnagel on toward the line from Lubny to Mirgorod, while von Kleist's Armored Group 1 was to attack Poltava. The OKW, however, countermanded von Rundstedt and reversed the two armies' missions, in order to complete the encirclement as quickly as possible. That decision ensured that Armored Group 1 would become involved in closing and holding the ring, rather than exploiting eastward, which meant that Army Group South would advance more slowly than planned once the encirclement was complete. In the short term, however, the battle was going very much in the Wehrmacht's favor. Von Kleist attacked out of the Dnieper bridgehead on 12 September, and his force met up with Guderian's at the town of Lovitsa three days later. A nearer encirclement cut off Kiev, which fell at last on 19 September. By 26 September most of the fighting in the pocket was over. The Red Army had been unable to stop the German advance, and Stalin had waited far too long – until 17 September – to give his permission for a withdrawal. When all was said and done, the Germans claimed to have captured the astounding total of 665,000 Soviet soldiers, along with 3,018 artillery pieces, 884 tanks, and 418 antitank guns.

While the Germans were making such impressive gains in the northern Ukraine, Eleventh Army also began operations farther south, toward the Crimea. Progress was slow at first, as the Germans tried to expand their bridgehead at Berislav, but by 17 September they had reached the Black Sea and the Sea of Azov, thus flanking the Crimean peninsula (see map 4). That success, together with the victory farther north, led the German high command to believe that Army Group South could take the Crimea and enter the Caucasus with minimal forces while Operation *Typhoon* – the attack on Moscow – went forward. To that latter end, von Rundstedt had to give up significant forces to von Bock. On 21 September a reduced and reorganized Army Group South received orders to take the Crimea and the eastern Ukraine, and to prepare to move into the Caucasus by crossing the Kerch Strait and the Don River. As part of this plan, Armored Group 1 would attack southeast from around Kremenchug along the Dnieper, then eastward toward Rostov on the Don River. Eleventh Army would take the Crimea and also advance along the northern coast of the Sea of Azov. Seventeenth Army would take Kharkov as well as thrusting eastward through Voroshilovgrad and on into the Don bend in the direction of

Stalingrad. And Sixth Army would cover the northern flank with a drive through Belgorod to the Don near Pavlovsk. Most of these advances involved distances of up to three hundred miles; apparently the Germans expected minimal resistance.

Army Group North: Operations in September

Army Group North also stayed on the offensive in this period, but von Leeb's expectation of quick success on the Leningrad front proved mistaken. Autumn weather comes early to that part of the world, which is on the same latitude as southern Alaska. Heavy rains, combined with continued stubborn resistance on the part of the Red Army, prevented von Leeb's forces from gaining much ground in the first week of September. Hitler, however, still believed that Army Group North would be able to cut off Leningrad within a few days, so on 5 September he ordered von Leeb's mobile forces and an entire air corps transferred to Army Group Center for the attack on Moscow, effective 15 September. Von Leeb protested the order to the OKH; by this point he saw that the loss of those units would leave him unable to establish a close blockade around the city, and thus the Soviets would be able to maintain their defense indefinitely. Halder, who knew that the attack on Moscow could not proceed before the end of September in any case, reluctantly agreed that von Leeb might hold on to his forces for the time being.

On 6 September von Leeb issued new orders to his armies. Sixteenth Army would carry out limited attacks south of Lake Ilmen and then go on the defensive in that sector, while one motorized corps drove north to Lake Ladoga. Armored Group 4, meanwhile, would make the main thrust toward Leningrad itself (see map 3). Initially the plan worked; Sixteenth Army reached Lake Ladoga, cutting off Leningrad's last land link, and Armored Group 4 managed to cut off some Soviet forces in the area south of the Neva River. Soviet counterattacks continued to be a problem, however. On 12 September von Leeb agreed that he could return the borrowed units of Armored Group 3 on 15 September, as ordered, but he asked to be allowed to keep Armored Group 4, since Leningrad seemed within his reach. For the moment he got a reprieve, but soon the OKH began taking away his mobile forces. On 22 September the Soviets launched strong attacks across the Neva, and two days later von Leeb concluded that his forces could no longer advance; the enemy had become too strong. Even the possibility of holding on to the army group's gains looked doubtful.

By the end of the month, Army Group North's front had quieted, and the various headquarters discussed how best to proceed against Leningrad. The Germans lacked the strength to take it; the army group proposed that the city would have to be forced to surrender through aerial bombardment and starvation. Likewise, Halder had admitted as early as 18 September that 'the situation will remain tight until such time when hunger takes effect as our ally.'³ Hitler and the OKW took that line of reasoning a step further. They did not envision accepting the city's surrender that year, even if offered, since that would mean that the Wehrmacht would be responsible for feeding the population. Instead, the OKW's recommendation was to wear the city down with terror and hunger, then open a few passages for women, children, and the elderly, who would be deported to the interior of Russia or allowed to scatter across the country. In the spring Leningrad could be occupied and the survivors likewise shipped east before the Germans leveled the city with explosives. For the moment, however, there seemed little hope of a quick solution through hunger, especially since some supply channels, such the water route across Lake Ladoga, were still open. Stalemate had settled in on the northern front; the decision in the campaign would have to come elsewhere.

Planning *Typhoon*

On 6 September Hitler issued a directive for the continuation of operations against Moscow. Defeat of the enemy in the north and south would have to come first, but once that had been accomplished, units could concentrate to eliminate what Hitler called 'Army Group Timoshenko,' after the Soviet commander in the sector in front of the capital. The Führer stipulated that the initial attack by two armored thrusts would aim for the area of Vyazma, well short of Moscow. Only after the Soviet forces in that pocket had been eliminated could the drive on the city begin. On 10 September the OKH issued its own directive, and as he had so often in the past, Halder did his best to get around Hitler's wishes, even while he formulated the order in such a way as to give the appearance of congruity. He assigned a lesser priority to defeating Army Group Timoshenko and instead called for a broader attack against Moscow, and sooner than Hitler had stipulated. He also accelerated the tempo and increased the scale of unit transfers from the northern and southern army groups. Such transfers would prove difficult, though, Halder's wishes notwithstanding. Many units remained tied down east of Kiev and in front of Leningrad longer than he planned.

Von Bock complained to Halder about the plan of attack on 13 September; he considered that an encirclement that closed near Vyazma would be too limited to achieve decisive results. Halder told him not to take the designation of Vyazma as an objective too seriously; he was determined not to allow that plan to interfere with the advance on Moscow. Four days later von Bock submitted his operation plan to Halder, and the two men worked together to ensure that the other army groups would transfer the necessary units to the center as early as possible, in spite of the local commanders' pleas. On the 19 September the OKH designated the attack Operation *Typhoon*, and on 24 September von Brauchitsch and Halder met with von Bock and his subordinate commanders and staff officers for the last major conference before the attack. They judged that the offensive could go forward, despite the lateness of the season, in the belief that the superiority of Germany's men and machines would be sufficient to ensure victory.

On 26 September Army Group Center issued its final orders to the armies (see map 6). Fourth Army, with Armored Group 4, would form the southern pincer, attacking north and south of the road running from Roslavl to Moscow and then wheeling inward toward the Smolensk-Moscow highway at Vyazma. The northern pincer would consist of Ninth Army, with Armored Group 3; it would jump off from the area between the Smolensk-Moscow highway and Belyy, advancing to the railroad line from Vyazma to Rzhev. Second Army would cover Fourth Army's southern flank while advancing toward Sukhinichi and Meshcohvsk; it would also take the industrial area around Bryansk if the opportunity presented itself. Armored Group 2 would open its attack two days before the other units, in order to gain the line from Orel to Bryansk as quickly as possible and then turn the Soviet position on the Desna River.

The Wehrmacht's leaders approached this plan with their usual confidence, without any apparent appreciation for how difficult their logistical situation had become. The continuous fighting since June had taken its toll; the pause to rest and refit that the original plan called for had never really happened. Losses were not being made up. At the beginning of September, for example, 30 per cent of the eastern army's tanks were total losses, and another 23 per cent were far to the rear, being overhauled. Such losses exceeded production by a significant margin, but even those tanks that Germany produced did not go to the front, because Hitler held them back to form new units. In total, the eastern army had lost 1,488 armored vehicles by the end of August and had received only 96 replacements. Only 34 per cent of Army Group Center's tanks were combat ready. Armored Group 2 was in an especially precarious position, because its foray into the Ukraine, followed by the return trip to the center of the front, wore out many of its vehicles and depleted its supplies. The other armies were somewhat better off, but they had also been fighting hard against the latest Soviet counteroffensive.

Now the push was on to prepare for the new attack. The supply and transportation services worked flat out to make up the shortages, but their efforts fell well short. The railroads were still delivering far less than the army needed, and the motor convoy system for getting the supplies from the railheads to the front was breaking down. By the end of September the shortfall in motor vehicles had reached an estimated 22 per cent, and that rate would only increase, given the number of different truck types (many of them civilian models), shortages of tires and spare parts, and the rough road conditions. In some armies the statistics were even worse: Armored Group 4, for example, lacked about half its trucks after its operations with Army Group North. The result was a shortfall in nearly every category of supply. By the beginning of October, Army Group Center had enough fuel on hand to carry it less than two hundred miles, barely the distance to Moscow, and the stocks of some types of ammunition would only suffice for less than two weeks' fighting. If the offensive dragged on, as it was almost certain to do, the armies would find themselves running out of the materials they needed. And then there was the winter to worry about; winter supplies would have to start moving forward from the depots on the border by November at the latest, if they were to reach the front in time. There is no evidence, however, that any of the senior officers considered abandoning the operation and going over to the defensive. Wagner even told Halder, shortly before the offensive began, that the supply situation was satisfactory; as always in the Wehrmacht, logistics took second place to operations. Everything seemed to depend on this last attack: one more short push, the army's leaders believed, would bring them the victory that had eluded them thus far. Given their supply status, it would have to.

Behind the Lines: Radicalization

The military operations of August and September were significant for Soviet prisoners and civilians in at least two ways. First, by conquering vast new stretches of territory and capturing yet more prisoners, the Wehrmacht increased its own burden; there was now more land to secure and exploit, longer supply lines to protect, and more potential enemies to control. Second, the fact that the Red Army and the Soviet government did not collapse, contrary to the Germans' confident pronouncements before the campaign, meant that the occupiers were probably even harsher toward some of their charges than they might otherwise have been. A partisan movement was beginning to make itself felt; the Germans' demands for food and labor increased; and the care of Soviet citizens, whether military or civilian, remained at the bottom of the Wehrmacht's ranking of priorities. Moreover, ideology worked in evil harmony with the military's more pragmatic motivations to further radicalize occupation policies.

There was no fundamental shift in German POW policy during this period, but there is no doubt that conditions for captured Soviet soldiers worsened. To begin with, the Commissar Order was still in effect and being applied widely. On 23 September the OKH passed along a request that the order be rescinded – not for any humanitarian reasons, but because of indications that the Soviets were resisting all the more fiercely because of it. Jodl passed the request on to Hitler, who refused to make any modifications. In fact, the shootings reached their peak during a four-month period ending in December. On 18 August the OKW had actually expanded the target list to include Politruks, the lowest-level political officers, after army units inquired as to their status. Further, on 8 September the OKW ordered all POW camp personnel to cooperate fully with the *Einsatzgruppen* in their efforts to cull Communists and Jews from the inmate population, contrary to the arrangement that Wagner had worked out with Heydrich in March and to his order of 24 July. Wagner resisted this idea at first, but by early October he was ready to go along with it. From that point forward, the SS was able to comb through the prisoner population freely, with help from the camps' administrative officers, and then either execute the victims locally or ship them to concentration camps to be killed later. A few such prisoners died in the first experiments with Zyklon B, the cyanide gas with which the Germans would later kill hundreds of thousands of Jews: the administration at Auschwitz tested a gas chamber for the first time on 3 September, using a group of Soviet POWs.

For the survivors of the various killing operations, conditions worsened as the summer went on, in part because many of them had already been in German captivity for weeks and were suffering cumulative effects. Prisoners who had experienced weeks-long foot marches with little food, only to arrive at open pens where both sustenance and shelter were lacking, continued to weaken over time. On 6 August the OKH's Army Administration Office issued the first central guidelines for the feeding of the POWs, guidelines that harped on some familiar themes. They stipulated that the prisoners be given only what was necessary, to avoid endangering morale on the home front by straining the food supply, and they further justified underfeeding the POWs by stating, again, that the Soviets had not signed the Geneva convention. In more specific terms, the guidelines called for rations totaling 2,040 calories per day for non-working prisoners and 2,200 calories per day for those who worked. Such rations would have been marginal even if they had actually been provided, but in most cases the prisoners received much less, and by the end of August they were already beginning to die in large numbers. In one region they were receiving no more than three hundred to seven hundred calories per day, and this at a time when the number of prisoners in the system was not yet great enough to create shortages. Organizational problems did add to the difficulties, but the root cause was simply a lack of concern. On the local level, no one wanted to take responsibility for feeding the POWs. At the policy level, Göring summed up the dominant attitude in a meeting with State Secretary Backe on 16 September, when he stated that

Germany was not bound by any international agreement to feed Soviet prisoners, and that their care would be measured only by their ability to work.

The Germans' own reports highlight the worsening situation in the camps. On 15 August the central labor office for the state of Saxony reported that POWs there were undernourished and incapable of performing much work. Another report, dated 11 September, indicated that in the Stalag at Lamsdorf the prisoners used their hands and cooking pots to dig holes in which to live, and ate grass, flowers, raw potatoes, and eventually their own dead. Dysentery and other diseases began to break out, but medical care was still almost nonexistent. The transfer camp in Molodecno reported a death rate in September of 1 per cent per day. Such rates became typical, and they would only increase as colder weather set in. Up to this point, however, there had been little effort to prepare the camps for winter. In occupied Poland, for example, preparation of winter quarters only began in September, and even then it went forward with little sense of urgency. The Germans provided almost no material for barracks, and as of the middle of the month there were only thirty-four trucks – and little fuel – available to help with the construction of housing for four to five hundred thousand prisoners. The Germans herded some prisoners into empty factories, prisons, and military barracks, but in many cases the state of these facilities was such that the prisoners were not much better off than they had been in their original camps.

The Partisan War and the German Reaction

As summer moved toward fall, the Soviet partisan movement was organizing itself, albeit slowly. The Soviet authorities had not prepared for guerrilla warfare before *Barbarossa* began. The Red Army's planners had assumed that massive counterattacks would push any invaders back into their own territory almost immediately, and so there seemed no need to consider any resistance on the part of the Soviet population. In addition, Stalin's paranoia about outside influences and his distrust of his own people created an atmosphere in which no one dared prepare for a foreign occupation. When the war did not progress as planned, however, the Soviets began organizing resistance cells in occupied lands and even in areas that the Germans would soon conquer. At this early date there were shortages of everything: explosives, weapons, radios, and other equipment, as well as trained leaders and fighters. More important, those Communist-led partisan bands that did exist found that few citizens were interested in supporting them; some civilians were collaborating with the Germans, some supported independent resistance movements, and most others simply wanted to keep a low profile. Still, the Germans were aware of the partisans' attempts to organize, and they reacted savagely. On 16 September Keitel issued an order entitled 'Communist Resistance Movement in the Occupied Territories.' It stated that there was 'in growing measure a danger for the German conduct of the war' and that the Führer had ordered that the military intervene 'everywhere with the sharpest measures,' because those taken up to that point had proven insufficient. Every attack was to be interpreted as springing from Communist sources, no matter what the circumstances. For every German life taken, the order called for the execution of fifty to one hundred 'Communists' – and the executions were to be carried out in ways that would further heighten the population's terror.[4]

Red Army troops, whether captured or still roaming free behind the lines, constituted a prime target for the antipartisan campaign. Up until late September, the Germans were still holding most Soviet POWs in the east, in part on the assumption that the campaign would be over before winter and in part simply because the Germans did not like the idea of sending thousands of Slavs into the homeland. Priorities began to change, however, as the number of POWs mounted. On 23 September the OKW authorized the transfer of a further half million prisoners to the Reich. The Germans did not do so because they wanted to make use of the POWs in industry; that measure would come later. At this point they feared that the swelling numbers of prisoners would lead to mass escapes, which in turn would feed into the partisan movement. For the same reason, the Wehrmacht moved quickly to eliminate Soviet stragglers and bypassed Red Army units. The commander of the Army Group Center rear area, for example, decreed on 11 August that all Red Army stragglers who did not turn themselves in by 15 August were to be treated as guerrillas, that is, shot on capture (he later extended the deadline to 31 August). Likewise, the OKH issued a central order on 13 September that any Soviet forces that were found to have reorganized themselves behind the lines were to receive the same treatment.

Soviet civilians found themselves caught between the emerging partisan movement and the Germans. The former demanded food, shelter, and sometimes labor, and often tortured and murdered anyone who worked with the occupiers. The latter, of course, demanded information on the partisans and punished anyone suspected of supporting them – while also retaining the Soviets' collective economic system and taking food in quantities guaranteed to produce starvation. (In fact, the system of collective farms was perfect from the German point of view; it gave them, as it had given the Soviet government, first claim on production.) In his 16 September meeting with Backe, Göring laid out his priorities for food distribution: the fighting troops first, then noncombatant troops in the occupied territories, then the troops at home, then the German civilian population, and finally the civilians in the occupied lands – but only those who worked for the occupiers. Rations on the home front, he insisted, must not only be maintained but increased; that way morale and the war effort would not suffer. He believed that knowledge of German prosperity would demoralize the enemy – but it simply fed resentment within the subject population.

The War against the Jews Expands

August and September marked a period of change in the German campaign to eradicate the Jews. Not only did the killing squads begin shooting ever greater numbers of victims, but they now included whole communities, rather than killing mostly young men. Whereas the killing of women and children had been merely allowed before, now it was encouraged and even ordered. The reasons for that change, and its timing, are still subject to debate. Some historians believe that Hitler made the decision to eradicate the Jews completely before the campaign even started, and that only tactical considerations, such as a shortage of shooters, limited the killing in the first few weeks. Others maintain that he decided on extermination while the campaign was going on and communicated it to the units in the field through Himmler. Still others emphasize the role of the field commanders themselves in instigating actions that Himmler and Hitler then approved and encouraged. There is no way to settle the debate with any degree of certainty – we have no written order, for example, and the various testimonies and other pieces of evidence are often contradictory. We can safely say, however, that whether the impetus for the killings came from the top down, the bottom up, or some combination of the two, there was no lack of enthusiasm at any level. Hitler was fully informed and certainly approved of the new measures, at the very least. Himmler made inspection tours to observe and encourage the men and their commanders, and often the killings increased in scale after his visits. He emphasized on several occasions that the men were doing an unpleasant but necessary job, and that he and the Führer accepted full responsibility. The Higher SS and Police Leaders and the military coordinated the activities of the *Einsatzgruppen*, the Order Police, and the other units that participated in the killings. And the *Einsatzgruppen* commanders themselves exercised considerable initiative in the choice of targets.

In explaining the killings, the Germans continued to invoke the idea that the Jews were linked to Communism and the partisan movement. In an order of 12 September, Keitel called for 'relentless and energetic measures, above all against the Jews as well, the main carriers of Bolshevism.'[5] When German forces rounded up and shot 'Communists' in accordance with the OKW order of 16 September, or when units launched 'antipartisan' campaigns, Jews constituted the majority of the victims. In any case, the link with the partisan war remained only the topmost layer in the Nazis' hierarchy of rationales, and we may never know precisely how their motives related to one another. The results, however, are plain. The *Einsatzgruppen*, together with various civilian and military police units, other SS formations, and army units, began to systematically annihilate the Jews of the Soviet Union. In some areas, local auxiliaries also assisted in the process. In the Baltic states and the western Ukraine, especially, auxiliaries registered victims, made arrests, and escorted prisoners to murder sites. At other times they carried out the killings, with and without German participation. (They only ran afoul of the Germans when they tried to call for independence, as in the case of one Ukrainian group, whose leaders the Germans arrested and shot.) All of this took place with the full knowledge and cooperation of the Wehrmacht's leaders.

The expanded killing program got off to an uneven start; some mass killings took place as early as late July, but the escalation did not reach its peak until the end of September. A full accounting of the killing actions would be impossible here, but a few examples will illustrate the scale of the destruction. On 18 and 26 August *Einsatzgruppe* B murdered two to three thousand Jews in Minsk – with Himmler in attendance at one of the shootings. Friedrich Jeckeln, the Higher SS and Police Leader in the south, used a police battalion and other units to kill 23,600 Jews in Kamanets-Podolskij between 28 and 31 August. On 11 September, *Einsatzgruppe* D killed three thousand men, women, and children in Dubossary. On the nineteenth, a unit of *Einsatzgruppe* C, in cooperation with an army field command headquarters, killed 3,145 Jews in Zhitomir. And between 18 and 20 September, another *Einsatzgruppe* C unit killed eighteen thousand Jews in Vinnitsa. These are only a few out of dozens of such incidents, some large, some small, but adding up to scores of thousands of victims in these two months alone, and representing an increase in the killing rate over the first phase of the campaign. In the second half of September, for example, *Einsatzgruppe* B alone raised its average daily kill rate from 290 to 420.

The Wehrmacht helped in these operations, as it had before, by providing supplies, transport and direction to the killing units, registering and marking Jews, sometimes assembling and guarding the victims and cordoning off the shooting sites, and in some cases taking part in the shootings themselves. Army Group South, in whose area of operations the greatest numbers of Jews lived, serves as a ready example of the kind of role that the army played in the killing campaign. Its relationship with *Einsatzgruppe* C was a close one. Von Reichenau's Sixth Army headquarters maintained daily communications with the *Einsatzgruppe* subunits operating in its area and helped to organize massacres. Von Reichenau himself issued an order on 10 August in which he defended the 'necessary executions of criminal, Bolshevik, mostly Jewish elements' that the SS was carrying out.[6] Seventeenth Army, under von Stülpnagel, took a less direct approach but did place an SS liaison official with the army's intelligence officer, and it also offered suggestions for inciting pogroms. The commander of the army group rear area, Karl von Roques, released numerous antisemitic orders and controlled the army units that took part in the shootings. On the SS side, the Security Police always tried to talk with local or regional military commands before major actions. Often the army itself requested shootings, especially of the mentally or physically handicapped in local institutions. One *Einsatzgruppe* subunit alone murdered over 1,200 ill people in Dnepropetrovsk.

Events surrounding the fall of Kiev provided the background for the most egregious case of army-SS cooperation. The Germans faced serious security issues in the newly conquered city. The Soviets had taken or destroyed all the valuable material they could, and had left booby traps and remote-controlled bombs behind in buildings the

Germans might use as headquarters or barracks. Searches revealed many of the bombs, but on 24 September one started a fire that spread through a large section of the city and lasted for five days. A colonel of the General Staff died in the incident, along with many other German soldiers, and Hitler himself ordered retribution. Some Jews and suspected partisans were shot right away. Meanwhile, a subunit of *Einsatzgruppe* C, commanded by Paul Blobel, arrived in the city to take up its work. The local army commandant, General Kurt Eberhard, held discussions with Blobel and the commander of *Einsatzgruppe* C, Otto Rasch, on a plan to eradicate the city's Jewish population. Eberhard's headquarters notified the Jews that they were to report on 29 September for 'resettlement.' When they reported, the Germans drove them out to a place called Babi Yar, where Blobel's unit, together with the staff of Higher SS and Police Leader Friedrich Jeckeln, three different police battalions, and Wehrmacht troops, shot them: 33,771 in all, in the course of two days. These events also had wider repercussions: they strengthened Hitler's determination not to allow German troops to take Leningrad or Moscow, but rather to level them and kill or scatter their inhabitants.

One should note, for the sake of context, that this was also a time when plans were moving forward for a broader Holocaust. On 10 September Himmler met with several key subordinates, apparently to draw up plans for the camps at Belzec, Majdanek, and Auschwitz/Birkenau in Poland. The experiments with Zyklon B at Auschwitz have already been mentioned. By midmonth Hitler had decided to empty the Reich of Jews as soon as possible; the initial plan was to ship them all to ghettos in occupied Poland but, although no written order exists, the evidence indicates that the decision for their physical extermination had probably already been made. Moreover, by September the SS was developing the carbon monoxide poisoning techniques with which they would kill hundreds of thousands of Jews and other victims in the east, building upon the Nazis' earlier experience in killing handicapped Germans. On about the eighteenth of that month a team in Mogilev field-tested a gas chamber that used car exhaust; the subjects were mentally ill Russians. From those experiments the killers developed mobile gas vans, which the *Einsatzgruppen* soon put to use. The experiments took place in part because the shootings in the east were becoming too widely known, and in part because the Germans were seeking a method of execution that would be easier on the killers; the members of the killing squads were having difficulty coping with the stress of shooting tens of thousands of people at point-blank range.

One looks almost in vain for any protest at these developments from the army's upper echelons. In early July von Leeb had spoken up against the pogroms, but Hitler had told him, if not in so many words, to mind his own business. 'We have no influence over these measures. The only thing left is to hold oneself at a distance,' von Leeb wrote in his diary.[7] Von Bock seems to have been attempting the same moral sleight of hand when, during Hitler's visit to his headquarters on 4 August, he made an appeal on behalf of the 'friendly and cooperative population.' He then forwarded a request to Arthur Nebe, the head of *Einsatzgruppe* B, that executions in Army Group Center's area should be carried out 'only when armed bandits or criminals are involved.'[8] Von Bock reportedly heard back that Nebe had agreed, but he had to be either willfully ignorant or misinformed if he believed it. *Einsatzgruppe* B, like the other killing units, continued to murder Jews in growing numbers – men and women, children and the elderly – whether or not there was any link to partisan or criminal activity, beyond the connection that the Nazis assumed to exist. And in only these few cases do we see any sign of reluctance on the part of senior German commanders. The rest either supported the policy wholeheartedly or decided, like von Leeb, to hold themselves at a distance.

By the end of September the tone of the war in the east was clear to both sides, and that tone was shaping the military outcome. This was no ordinary campaign. Most Soviet citizens could see that the Germans were out to destroy the USSR as a state and kill or enslave its people. Most Germans, for their part, saw plenty in the Soviet Union to confirm what the Nazis' propaganda had said all along, or at least they interpreted what they saw to match their preconceptions, and many of them dropped any pretense of restraint. This is not to say that no one acted honorably. In general, however, *Barbarossa* had become a war of annihilation, and that fact worked more to the Soviets' advantage than to the Germans'. As more Soviet civilians and soldiers came to recognize the Nazi regime's true nature and goals, they fought all the harder. Behind the lines, the Germans were rapidly destroying any chance they might have had to gain significant support for a crusade against the Stalinist state, but they could not or would not see the effect their policies were having. At the front, meanwhile, German brutality was helping to inspire the Red Army to fanatical resistance. Given that fact, plus the Soviets' ability to come up with a seemingly endless succession of new units, the Germans' prospects for imposing a military solution were disappearing even faster than their political opportunities. Time and strength remained in 1941 for one last lunge, but the outlook was already all but hopeless.

5

The Final Drive on Moscow and Systematic Killing, October to December

On the night of 1–2 October, the eve of their renewed offensive against Moscow, German soldiers heard an address from their Führer. In part he said:

> In these 3½ months, my soldiers, *the conditions have finally been created for the last colossal stroke*, which still, *before the onset of winter, should crush this enemy*. . . . Today is the beginning of the last great battle of decision in this year. You will strike this enemy a crushing blow, and with him also the instigator of this war, England itself. . . . We will remove, from the German Reich and from the whole of Europe, a threat that has not hung over the continent more horribly since the times of the Huns and, later, of the Mongol storms.[1]

Hitler was right on one point: this would be the last major battle of the year, and thus of the campaign; neither the time nor the resources existed for anything more. As to its outcome, on that point the Führer's prediction would prove disastrously wrong. In the coming offensive the Wehrmacht would again demonstrate its technical and tactical superiority, and would win an initial victory greater than any that preceded it. As had happened before, however, in the end that victory would not be enough, and Germany's army would find itself overextended and vulnerable, about to taste real defeat for the first time.

Vyazma and Bryansk

The Germans had marshaled more than 1.9 million men in seventy-eight divisions for Operation *Typhoon*, with fourteen thousand artillery pieces, over one thousand tanks, and nearly 1,400 combat aircraft. They faced 1.25 million Soviet soldiers, with 7,600 artillery pieces, nearly one thousand tanks, and over six hundred aircraft. The Soviet units, though, were a mix of exhausted and green troops. Only forty-five of the tanks in the central sector were new models. There were shortages of every kind of equipment. Communications were slow and tenuous, the command system cumbersome, confused, and uncertain. Defensive lines were only 40–50 per cent complete. Although the Germans were also weaker than their numbers might indicate, on the whole they held a considerable edge.

Armored Group 2 opened the offensive on 30 September, with two thrusts from a starting point near Sostka (see map 6). The right-hand of these aimed straight northeast for Orel. The other would loop around to the northwest after its initial penetration and take Bryansk, in cooperation with Second Army attacking eastward. The first day's progress was good; the spearheads advanced approximately fifteen miles into the Soviet defenses. On the next day the Red Army counterattacked, but it failed to halt Guderian, whose tanks broke through into the Soviets' rear. On 3 October the Germans took Orel, having advanced over 130 miles in four days. The advance was so swift that the city had had no chance to prepare a defense; in fact the streetcars were still running when the Germans arrived. On the left, the Germans captured Bryansk on 7 October, trapping a large Soviet force.

Farther north, Armored Groups 3 and 4 began their drives on 2 October. They caught the Soviets, who were concentrating their attention on Guderian's thrust and thought it the main attack, fully unaware. Hoth's and Hoepner's tanks quickly penetrated the Soviet defenses, and the Red Army was unable to shift sufficient forces in time to stop them. By the end of the next day, some units had advanced fifty miles. With the two wings closing in on Vyazma, the Soviet commanders pressed Stalin to allow a withdrawal, but he refused until 5 October, too late to save the enormous force within the pocket. By 7 October the wings had linked up. Armored Group 3's mobile forces had to halt because of supply problems, and so some Soviet forces escaped over the next few days, albeit with heavy losses. Still, the haul was staggering: approximately six hundred thousand more Soviet troops fell into German hands, in addition to the more than eighty-five thousand in the encirclement at Bryansk.

The Momentum Fades

The outstanding results of less than two weeks of fighting put the German leaders into high spirits, as one might expect. The Soviets had lost approximately one million men, most of them killed, missing, or captured. They had, at least for the moment, no strategic reserves with which to plug a gap more than three hundred miles wide. Hitler announced as early as 3 October that the enemy was broken and would never rise again. On 5 October General Wagner wrote:

> the last great collapse stands immediately before us. . . . Operational goals are being set that earlier would have made our hair stand on end. Eastward of Moscow! Then I estimate that the war will be mostly over, and perhaps there really will be a collapse of the [Soviet] system. . . . I am constantly astounded at the Führer's military judgment. He intervenes in the course of operations, one could say decisively, and up until now he has always acted correctly.[2]

And two days later Halder opined that, with 'reasonably good direction of battle and moderately good weather,' Army Group Center would be able to complete the encirclement of Moscow.[3] Just at this point, however, the Germans began to encounter serious obstacles and to make some mistakes, both of which would hinder their advance.

To begin with, the Wehrmacht's leaders apparently concluded that the Soviets could no longer mount any effective defense in front of Moscow. Rather than concentrate their forces for a determined drive on the capital, the Germans aimed at achieving several different objectives simultaneously. Armored Group 3 received orders to advance northward toward Kalinin, in an effort, together with elements of Ninth and Sixteenth armies, to deal with Soviet forces facing Army Group North. Armored Group 4 was to sweep around to the north of Moscow and prepare for a further advance in the direction of Yaroslavl and Rybinsk; Fourth Army would operate on its right. Second Armored Army (formerly Armored Group 2; it was renamed on 5 October) was not only to send one arm northeast through Tula and around the southern side of Moscow, but was also to send another arm southeast to take Kursk; that move would give it a front of over two hundred miles. Moreover, all of these moves were to start while various units were still reducing the Soviet forces at Bryansk and Vyazma. Von Brauchitsch and Halder had agreed to begin the pursuit immediately, and not wait for the forces that were eliminating the pockets. Von Bock tried to oppose these new orders – he feared that the plan would disperse his forces too much – but to no avail.

Differences of opinion also began to show up over the fate of the largest Soviet cities. On 7 October Hitler ordered that, because of the losses that German troops had suffered from booby traps and bombs in Kiev, no troops would enter Moscow, Leningrad, or other major urban centers. Von Brauchitsch informed von Bock of that decision vis-à-vis Moscow the same day; he said that the Führer intended the Wehrmacht to put a ring around the city but not go in. The OKW issued an order on 12 October in which it stated that these cities were to be encircled and bombarded, and their inhabitants made to flee to the interior of Russia, the presumption being that they would be a burden on the Soviet authorities rather than the Germans. On 20 October the OKH issued its own version of the order, in which it stipulated that German troops were neither to fight fires in the city nor to give food to Soviet citizens. In the field, however, practical concerns made the implementation of the orders problematic. The army needed those cities: it needed the transportation lines that intersected in them, and it needed buildings for housing, supply storage, and headquarters. This was a conflict that the Germans never really resolved, except on a de facto basis. When Army Group South later took Kharkov, for example, it simply ignored the directives from on high. The facilities in the city were too valuable to do otherwise.

While the high command was making these broad decisions, events on the ground were taking a turn for the worse. For one thing, the autumnal rains had arrived, ushering in the season the Russians call the *rasputitsa*, literally the 'time without roads'; this development brought out the weaknesses in the Wehrmacht's logistical planning. Already by 8 October Army Group Center was having problems with mud and with alternating freezes and thaws that made travel difficult, while the inclement weather also grounded the Luftwaffe. By 12 October Second Armored Army was reporting that its units were averaging less than one mile per hour. Farther north, Soviet delayed-action bombs were disrupting traffic on the main highway out of Vyazma toward the front. The railways were not keeping up, and lateral supply routes were proving completely inadequate. Supplies were not reaching the fighting units in sufficient quantities. The armor was becoming separated from the infantry once again, and many units remained tied down at Bryansk and Vyazma. The advance was beginning to falter, the 'pursuit' turning into a slogging match against hastily assembled, but determined, Red Army forces. (One should note that, for all the Germans' postwar complaints about mud and cold, the Soviets faced the same conditions, yet they coped much better. The weather did not defeat the Germans: their failure to plan for it did.)

Hoth's Armored Group 3 began its drive north to Kalinin on 10 October, and actually made good progress; four days later it had torn another gap in the Soviet defenses and taken the city, but the Soviets kept the pressure up against the isolated spearhead. Ninth Army, on the left, took Rzhev and prepared to continue north; on 18 October, however, it warned that it would not be able to advance much farther without a long pause to resupply and refit. Fourth Army, on Hoth's right, advanced to the line from Volokolamsk through Mozhaysk to Kaluga, where it ran short of supplies at the same time as it met resistance from strongly entrenched Soviet forces; it would remain stuck on or just east of that line for the next two weeks. Guderian's left wing got as far as Mtsensk and Bolkhov before it, too, stalled in heavy fighting. It hoped to renew its advance on 20 October, but only if the road conditions were good enough, and that looked unlikely. In fact the roads were continuing to worsen. Vehicles and horses alike stuck fast in deep mud; hundreds of miles sometimes separated the fighting troops from their supply convoys; fuel, food, and ammunition were not getting through. Moreover, by 16 October the army group's losses had reached 277,000, while it had received only 151,000 replacements.

Hitler and the OKH reacted to the deteriorating situation with still greater demands, which seem to indicate, at the very least, that the people at the top did not understand the situation. The OKH, despite clear signs to the contrary, apparently feared most of all that the Soviets would withdraw, leaving nothing but scorched earth behind them, and rebuild their strength for operations in the spring. On October 16 the OKH directed that all army groups form special pursuit detachments, give them plenty of fuel (if possible), and send them after distant objectives, in order to engage enemy units before they could pull back. Three days later the OKH instructed von Bock to gather strong mobile forces in the area of Kalinin and Torzhok for a thrust northward into the Valday Hills, which Halder wanted taken before winter. An advance to Rybinsk and beyond would follow. This was pure fantasy; von Bock's forces would barely have been able to cover that distance unopposed. As of 22 October, however, the OKH was still insisting on such a maneuver.

Developments on the Flanks

In the meantime, the flanking army groups were also under pressure to make progress. In the north, von Leeb was trying to establish a stable front around Leningrad. Hitler proposed on 3 October that he thrust northeast from Chudno to Tikhvin, thus linking up with the Finns, cutting off the route by which the Soviets were transporting supplies to the edge of Lake Ladoga and on into Leningrad, and also isolating the Soviet troops facing the more northern part of the front along the Volkhov River. Von Leeb objected that he lacked sufficient forces, and at that moment the pressure on the army group's front also weakened because of the fighting around Moscow, so the idea was put on hold. The senior leaders apparently hoped that the Soviets might give up on Leningrad entirely and withdraw further to the east. Within ten days, though, the OKH decided that the operation would have to go forward after all, and on 16 October von Leeb's forces attacked. The going was extremely slow, due to rain, snow, mud, and fierce Soviet resistance; a week into the offensive the spearhead had advanced less than halfway to Tikhvin. The enemy was most definitely not withdrawing. By 25 October the attack had nearly ground to a halt. Ironically, Hitler wanted to stop the operation, but von Leeb persuaded him to let the attack continue.

In Army Group South's area, the attacks that began in late September made slow progress at first (see map 7). Eleventh Army, now under General Erich von Manstein, ran into tough resistance and suffered heavy losses in its effort to enter the Crimean peninsula. Armored Group 1 also found the going hard at the start, but by 1 October it had taken Zaporozhye, and from there it headed east.

The Soviets saw that this drive threatened to meet up with Eleventh Army's advance along the Sea of Azov, and attempted to pull back. They were a bit too late, and the Germans encircled six divisions near Berdyansk before continuing on to Mariupol. By 11 October Armored Group 1 had reached the Mius River north of Taganrog, but within a few days bad weather, supply problems, exhaustion, and vehicle breakdowns halted von Kleist's advance. In the northern part of the sector, the Soviets effectively blunted Seventeenth Army's initial attack out of the Krasnograd-Poltava area, while Sixth Army proved too weak to protect Seventeenth's left flank or maintain contact with Army Group Center. On 1 October Hitler ordered that the attack on the Donets basin would be the top priority; Kharkov would have to wait for the time being. On 6 October, von Reichenau and von Stülpnagel renewed their attacks, forcing the Red Army to retreat past Bogoduchov and Lozovaya in the course of the next few days, but by 12 October the attacks stalled again as a result of the familiar combination of weather and exhaustion.

With their forces in the south largely stuck in place, Hitler and his commanders tried to decide what to do next. On 14 October Hitler ordered forces from Seventeenth Army diverted to the north, to meet Sixth Army's drive and encircle Soviet forces west of Kharkov. That plan threatened von Stülpnagel's advance to the southeast into the Donets basin, and for three days Hitler, the OKH, and von Rundstedt wrangled before the Führer dropped the idea. The high command then agreed that von Manstein would renew his attack on the Crimea, while First Armored Army (formerly Armored Group 1), Seventeenth Army, and Sixth Army would move straight east to occupy all the territory up to the Don River and even establish bridgeheads across it in the direction of Stalingrad. Here too the Germans decided that the Soviets would withdraw in front of the advancing Wehrmacht troops, despite earlier experiences to the contrary.

Von Manstein opened his attack on the Crimea on 18 October, but his forces, which lacked armored support, fared badly at first against prepared defenses in the narrow neck of land leading into the peninsula. Not until 28 October did the Soviet defenses collapse, and von Manstein's troops went on to occupy almost the whole of the Crimea; only a small area around the fortress city of Sevastopol held out. As for the other armies, von Rundstedt finally had to recognize that their situations did not allow for the kind of ambitious objectives that the last set of orders had laid out. On 25 October his headquarters told von Reichenau (whose forces had just taken Kharkov at last) to advance as far as Belgorod, von Stülpnagel to gain a bridgehead over the Donets at Izyum, and von Kleist to carry on to Rostov. After that the troops would lay in supplies and wait for the ground to freeze before attempting any further advances.

Reality Intrudes – To an Extent

The situation in the last half of October finally brought home to some members of the high command that the campaign was not going to end as planned. On 20 October Wagner, who predicted victory so confidently not three weeks before, wrote to his wife, 'It can't be kept a secret any longer: we are hung up in the muck, in the purest sense.' Then on 24 October he wrote: 'In my opinion it is not possible to come to the end [of this war] this year; it will still last a while. The how? is still unsolved.'[4] On the same day Friedrich Paulus, a senior officer with the General Staff, announced to an assembly of other staff officers that plans to drive through the Caucasus into Iran, with the objective of eventually threatening the British position in the Middle East, would have to wait until spring. Hitler himself admitted to von Brauchitsch that Germany could no longer hope to reach the farthest objectives, such as Murmansk, the Volga River, and the Caucasus oil fields, in 1941. The new goal, once the ground froze, was to strike one more blow that would weaken the Soviets beyond hope of recovery in 1942, while also securing positions from which to complete the conquest of the USSR in the spring.

The dawning awareness of the eastern army's limits was not as complete as it might have been, however. The Germans' intelligence picture was overly optimistic, for one thing. They believed that the Soviets now had 160 divisions and forty separate brigades, most at below 50 per cent strength. Actually, on 1 November the Soviets had 269 divisions and sixty-five brigades, for a total of 2.2 million men, in their field forces and the strategic reserve. Experience, arms, and equipment were all still lacking, but in terms of raw numbers the Red Army was far from spent. The disparity between the image and reality goes far to explain the continuing lack of realism in the German leaders' expectations for the next phase of the campaign. For example, Halder told von Rundstedt's chief of staff that the army group's order to halt on the lower Don would create the wrong impression among the troops and might detract from efforts to reach Stalingrad in December, after the ground had frozen but before (he hoped) any heavy snowfall. Von Brauchitsch likewise urged von Rundstedt to try to reach both Stalingrad and the Maykop oil fields, which were nearly three hundred miles to the east and over two hundred to the south, respectively, of First Armored Army's most advanced positions. Von Rundstedt feared that further operations would leave his units ineffective for the coming spring, but von Brauchitsch did not believe that there would be any strong resistance east of the Don. (First Armored Army did open its advance toward Rostov on 5 November, but within two days heavy rains began and soon stopped it cold; ten days would pass before it could move again.)

Also on 7 November, Halder sent an announcement to the chiefs of staff of the army groups and armies, informing them that he was planning to hold a conference in the town of Orsha in about a week's time to discuss the situation. In the supporting paperwork he included a map with two boundaries drawn on it, to mark the 'farthest' and the 'minimum' advances for which the eastern army should strive. The 'minimum' boundary started from a point well east of Leningrad and ran southward, passing Moscow on the east by 160 miles, to Rostov. The 'farthest' boundary, which Halder believed must be the actual goal, extended the front another seventy-five to ninety miles eastward in the northern and central sectors, to cut off Murmansk and take the Vologda and Gorkii industrial areas, and included Stalingrad and Maykop in the southern sector. Such an advance would deprive the USSR of its oil and other important raw materials, as well as key railroad links and manufacturing centers.

The conference at Orsha took place on 13 November, and it must have been a disappointment for Halder. In that meeting, and in another that he held with his principal staff assistants on 23 November, he stated that he and the Führer were both inclined to pursue a strategy that, rather than simply conserving strength, would aim for the maximum possible effect with the forces available. 'It is possible,' he said,

> that the war is shifting from the level of military success to the level of moral and economic endurance, without changing the military's mission, that is, to use all available means to damage the enemy as severely as possible. . . . The military power of Russia is no longer a danger for the reconstruction of Europe. . . . The enemy . . . is not yet destroyed. We will not achieve his full destruction in this year, despite the efforts of our troops, which cannot be recognized enough. What with the endlessness of the territory and its inexhaustible supply of manpower, we definitely cannot reach 100 per cent of that goal. Naturally we knew that from the start.[5]

At Orsha he argued initially that the army would have to take some risks so that it could reach the farthest boundary if possible, or at least the minimum boundary. The reaction from the other officers present, however, was universally negative. Even the planners from his own staff painted a bleak picture. There was no sign that the Soviets would run out of soldiers. Personnel losses on the German side totaled nearly seven hundred thousand. The fighting strength of the average Wehrmacht infantry division stood at 65 per cent; that of an armored division at only 35 per cent. The General Staff estimated that the eastern army's 136 major units had the fighting strength of only 83. The army groups delivered a litany of complaints regarding shortages of manpower, equipment, and supplies, and many expressed concern about the ability of the troops to fight on much longer. The transport system was in crisis; the frost had set in a week earlier for Army Group Center, but the damage to vehicles and locomotives from the cold did much to cancel out the improvement in road conditions. Efforts to stock up on ammunition and fuel for further attacks would mean that winter clothing, as well as construction materials for quarters and defensive positions, would remain in depots far to the rear. The representatives of Army Groups North and South wanted to stop their advances entirely; those from von Bock's staff could contemplate a push for Moscow, but nothing further.

That evening Halder summed up the results of the meeting. He admitted that his goals at the start had been too optimistic. Still, he wanted all three army groups to push on until mid-December, and he expected that Army Group Center would take Moscow, even if it did not get too far beyond it. He said he anticipated six weeks of cold but dry weather, from mid-November until the end of December, in which to carry out the operations. When Colonel Otto Eckstein, chief supply officer for Army Group Center, pointed out the precariousness of the supply situation, Halder clapped him on the back and replied, 'You are certainly right to be anxious, based on your calculations. But we don't want to hold Bock up, if he thinks he can do the thing; indeed it takes a little luck, too, to conduct a war.'[6] Here he expressed not just the continuing subordination of logistic considerations to the operational plan, but an unhealthy dose of wishful thinking. In fact von Bock's plan did not even project beyond a partial encirclement of Moscow, which would leave his forces exposed and vulnerable without achieving any strategic or operational benefit. Halder had already noted that 'the time for spectacular operational feats is past. . . . The only course lies in purposeful exploitation of tactical opportunities.'[7] Both men appear to have been hoping, again, that one more stroke would produce a Soviet collapse. Of that there was no sign, however; while the Germans were making their preparations, the Soviets were actually building defensive lines well to the east of their capital, as well as delivering their own attacks in the north and south that would prevent the Germans from reinforcing the offensive in the center.

Strain on the Flanks

In the far north, Sixteenth Army finally took Tikhvin on 8 November after two weeks of fighting (see map 6). Busch's forces also closed in on Volkhov from the south, in an effort to push the Soviets out of the area south of Lake Ladoga, but without success. The threat from the southeastern flank only grew as time went on, preventing Sixteenth Army from expanding its hold. Von Leeb's only hope was to draw forces from another part of his front, but without the leeway to eliminate the Soviet pocket on the coast west of Leningrad – which Hitler refused to allow him – he could not free up any additional troops. Then on 12 November the Soviets began a series of counterstrokes against that vulnerable front south of Tikhvin. The attacks were not well coordinated, and the Germans were able to beat them off, but the effort required that von Leeb transfer some forces from Tikhvin itself. On the nineteenth the Soviets attacked again, and the next day they were able to penetrate the Wehrmacht's lines. As the end of the month approached, von Leeb could see that he would be forced to abandon Tikhvin and set up a defensive line farther to the southwest.

In the south, too, the German offensives were running out of steam (see map 7). Rostov remained the center of attention. On 17 November von Kleist's forces resumed the offensive against the city in temperatures that dipped down to eight degrees below zero. Their thrust against Rostov from the northwest coincided with Soviet attacks against their eastern flank. The Soviets actually outnumbered the Germans in the sector, but the Soviet commander had not deployed his forces properly, so the counterattacks failed. First Armored Army went on to take the city on 20 November. The

Germans' ability to hold remained in doubt, however. The Soviets launched further attacks from the south and east in the following days, against a German force whose supply system was collapsing. Fuel shortages left the army's tanks nearly immobile. Already on 21 November, von Kleist's staff concluded that a withdrawal from the Don was inevitable unless significant reinforcements arrived, but they knew how unlikely that was. Sixth and Seventeenth armies were having their own problems at Belgorod and along the Donets; no help would be coming from that quarter. (In fact, Halder demanded that Sixth Army attack from east of Kharkov toward Kupyansk, in hopes of taking some pressure off von Kleist, but von Reichenau insisted that further attacks would be irresponsible.) Von Rundstedt's headquarters, meanwhile, continued to lay plans for advances to Stalingrad and Maykop, although the material basis for that planning is a mystery.

On 28 November the Soviets drove the Germans out of Rostov. A series of miscommunications then followed among Hitler, the OKH, Army Group South, and First Armored Army, as von Rundstedt approved von Kleist's planned withdrawal toward the Mius River. The Führer, who wanted the line held farther east, got the impression that von Rundstedt was defying him. Such was not really the case – the problem lay in poorly formulated reports – but Hitler relieved the army group commander on 1 December and replaced him with von Reichenau. The latter, however, proved no more able than his predecessor to hold an intermediate line, and Hitler finally had to approve the withdrawal after all. Meanwhile, the army group and the OKH continued to cling to the illusion that they would shortly resume the offensive toward Stalingrad and Maykop.

The Last Lunge toward Moscow

By the time Halder was delivering his summation at Orsha, the ground in Army Group Center's sector had frozen solid, allowing the attack to start again (see map 6). On 15 November, Ninth Army and Armored Group 3 resumed the offensive on Moscow's northern flank. Their orders were to attack to the Volga Reservoir and the Moscow-Volga Canal and then turn southward toward the city. At first they made good progress; they broke through south of the Volga Reservoir on November 18 and headed for Klin. On the southern flank, Second Armored Army picked up its attack that same day; its role was to swing north through Tula and Kolomna with two separate thrusts. Its right wing advanced around to the east of Tula, but the Soviets had launched strong attacks against the left wing as well as Fourth Army on 13 November. In one sense the Soviet spoiling offensive was a failure, in that it weakened the Soviets' defensive forces at a crucial moment. On the other hand, it forced the Germans onto the defensive; neither Second Armored Army's left wing nor Fourth Army could move forward, and the attack also held open a salient with Tula at its southern tip, a salient that threatened the inner flank of Second Armored Army's right wing. And with Second Army, on the army group's southern flank, advancing on a divergent course to the east toward Kursk and Voronezh, its forces were not close enough to support Guderian.

The balance of the month was a story of diminishing returns on the German side. By the time Guderian's tanks started their advance, von Brauchitsch already considered that the chances of reaching Moscow were fading. Halder, on the other hand, considered success a matter of willpower. On 20 November the OKH instructed von Bock to continue the attack on the wings, regardless of Fourth Army's situation. The circumstances appear to have put von Bock under severe strain. On the one hand he expressed agreement with Halder's view that the Soviets must be on the brink of collapse, and that victory would go to the side that held out the longest. On the other, he knew the state of his troops, and he protested that they did not have the strength to carry out the kind of envelopment that Halder had in mind. Guderian, too, reported that he would not be able to complete his assigned tasks because of the arrival of fresh

Soviet troops to his east. By this time, according to his calculations, his forces had only 150 tanks out of the 1,000 with which he had begun the campaign, and only 15 per cent of his unarmored motor vehicles were available. On November 21 he requested a change in the objectives for the operation, but when the request reached Halder three days later, he rejected it.

Halder's determination notwithstanding, the offensive was grinding to a halt. By 23 November, although Armored Group 3 had taken Klin, its advance was slowing. On 25 November von Bock ordered Second Armored Army to go on the defensive, except for continuing efforts to take Tula. On 27 November Wagner told Halder that the army was at the end of its strength. That same day the Soviets counterattacked at Tula and stymied the Wehrmacht's attempt to isolate the city, while on the northern wing Armored Group 3 had to abandon the only bridgehead it had established on the eastern shore of the Moscow-Volga Canal. On the twenty-ninth, von Bock informed Halder that unless a decision could be reached in the next few days, the attack would have to be called off; otherwise the situation could become a 'brutish, chest-to-chest struggle of attrition,' for which he would not accept responsibility.[8] The next day one of Hoepner's divisions got within artillery range of Moscow – some officers reported being able to see the spires of the city through their binoculars – but it would get no farther.

With the arrival of December, the Germans were neither able to press their attack home nor, seemingly, willing to confront their situation's full significance. Von Bock demanded on 1 December that the OKH either bring up reserves or, if none were available, allow him to withdraw to a more defensible line. Over the next few days, von Kluge, Guderian, and Hoepner all reported that they were breaking off their attacks; their troops were spent. And yet von Bock also told Jodl that he hoped to continue the advance. At this point the Germans had placed themselves in a bind; they could neither attack nor defend effectively, and now winter had begun. According to the original plan, by now the Soviets would have collapsed and most of the army would have been withdrawn; supplies and accommodations for only about fifty-six divisions would be needed. Instead, the entire eastern army was still locked in combat. Because of the decision to make the last thrust on Moscow, together with the inadequate state of the transportation network, all the winter clothing and construction materials, as well as reserves of fuel and ammunition, were still in depots far to the rear. Neither defensive positions nor cold weather quarters existed. Temperatures were dropping into the minus thirties Fahrenheit. Frostbite and hypothermia were becoming as great a threat as combat. Morale was sinking with the mercury.

At least, thought the Germans, the Soviets must also be on their last legs. On 4 December the eastern intelligence branch of the General Staff announced that the Soviets were not in a position to launch any significant attacks without bringing up reinforcements on a large scale. Unbeknownst to their foes, however, the Soviets had done exactly that. On 24 November the Soviet high command ordered the deployment of its strategic reserve, a force at least as large as that which the Germans attacked at the beginning of October. Moreover, many of the new divisions consisted of battle-tested Siberian troops: since learning, through a highly placed spy, that the Japanese were going to attack south and east into the Pacific, Stalin had felt free to release some of the forces he had stationed in the far eastern portion of the USSR. Soviet forces in the west now numbered 343 divisions and ninety-eight brigades: over four million men. The best estimate is that the Red Army had suffered more than two million casualties since the end of September, including over 750,000 killed, but it had fought the Wehrmacht to a standstill at last, and now it was about to turn the tables.

Behind the Lines

The Wehrmacht's difficulties in October and November 1941 made the situation for enemy civilians and prisoners of war still worse. The army's needs to secure its lines of supply, to feed itself, and to take advantage of civilian labor all became that much greater as the conflict continued and winter set in. The partisan threat was growing, and the Germans saw the hundreds of thousands of prisoners, stragglers, Communists, and Jews who remained in the occupied territories as the source of that threat. The occupiers' reaction remained what it had been before: a combination of cynical manipulation, malignant neglect, and murderous, ideologically driven brutality, all of which served, ultimately, to strengthen the Soviets' resistance rather than crush it.

In the case of the Soviet prisoners of war, a situation that was already horrible deteriorated still further. In this period the Germans made some fundamental policy changes that held the potential to improve the prisoners' lot, but perhaps their most illuminating decision was to launch a propaganda effort. The Wehrmacht Propaganda Office, part of the OKW, issued guidelines on 10 November, according to which the regime in Moscow was to be blamed for carrying out a scorched-earth campaign that was depriving the German army of the means to feed its prisoners. No one, the guidelines stated, could expect the Wehrmacht to transport food for prisoners while still engaged in combat. The fact that such an argument lacked any validity under international law was of no apparent importance to the authors. Doubtless they wanted to believe it, rather than recognize the reality behind the deaths of hundreds of thousands of their charges, which had little to do with the Soviets' scorched-earth campaign.

For thousands of those POWs, the end still came as a result of direct action on the part of the SS, with help from the army. On 7 October the OKH followed the example of the OKW and ordered that the *Einsatzgruppen* be allowed access to the prisoner-of-war camps in the OKH zone. The killing squads were to carry out their actions on their own responsibility and in close coordination with the camp commandants and local headquarters' intelligence officers. Soviet personnel would be released from POW status when they were turned over to the SS, thereby eliminating – at least according to a very narrow standard – the army's responsibility for them. The order did stipulate that the selections should take place 'as unobtrusively as possible' and that the liquidations should be carried out 'without delay and so far from the transit camps and towns that they will not become known to the remaining prisoners and the local residents.'[9] Heydrich followed this up with an order on 29 October to the *Einsatzgruppen*, in which he expanded the categories of prisoners to be shot and acknowledged the OKH's cooperation in formulating the new guidelines. Field Marshal von Bock apparently had some misgivings about this arrangement, but finally agreed that the selected prisoners be transferred to civilian camps outside the army group rear area, where they could then be 'dealt with as the political necessities and the security of the Reich require.'[10] Von Bock's neighbor to the south, von Rundstedt, was either less involved or less squeamish; the records of one *Einsatzgruppe* C subunit show that it killed 740 POWs at the Dulag (Durchgangslager, or transit camp) in Lozovaya and 1,109 Jewish Red Army soldiers at the Dulag in Borispol in early November.

In the first few weeks of autumn there was little sign that conditions for the remaining prisoners would improve. There were, for example, more than 112,000 POWs in Germany proper at the beginning of October, but they had arrived in such a poor state that those who could work at all – fewer than half – reached productivity levels that were barely 10–20 per cent of those that French POWs had attained earlier. The local authorities saw that only more food would help, but at first the military refused to provide it. Within the OKH zone, in fact, General Wagner ordered that prisoners performing manual labor, who had been receiving a little over half the food of German soldiers, were to suffer a further cut. Moreover, Wagner's order stipulated that all prisoner rations would have to come from the surrounding territory; the army would not be responsible for transporting food for its captives. Some combat divisions also ordered that POWs be stripped of any clothing that would help protect Wehrmacht soldiers from the cold. That order was in part a result of the high command's decision to bring up ammunition and fuel for continued offensive operations, rather than the winter uniforms the troops needed.

At the end of October a policy shift occurred that should have improved conditions. On the last day of the month, Hitler ordered, through Keitel, that Soviet prisoners of war be used extensively within the German war economy. Labor shortages on the home front were hurting production – over 1.5 million positions stood empty – and the dawning realization that the war would not end in 1941 meant that the soldiers of the eastern army would not be demobilized to fill the ranks of workers any time soon, while wartime production demands would, if anything, increase. That economic argument was strong enough to persuade Hitler to reverse his earlier decision and allow more Slavs into the Fatherland.

In the wake of that decision, the German authorities finally began to revise their food policies; the order had even stated that 'a prerequisite for working ability is adequate feeding.'[11] Rations for working Soviet POWs in Germany had already been raised, actually: they were supposed to get the same rations as other nations' prisoners, aside from meats and fats, of which they would receive half. (Rations for nonworking POWs were reduced further.) In mid-November the OKH ordered supplemental food for its prisoners, and on 26 November it ordered a systematic increase in rations, which it made permanent on 2 December. The new norm would be 2,335 calories per day – 2,570 for prisoners performing hard labor – and exhausted prisoners would receive supplemental rations to renew their strength. The OKW, meanwhile, ordered that its prisoners be sorted into three groups, according to working ability: those who were fully capable, those whose capability was subject to improvement with care, and those who were permanently incapable. The first group would receive normal rations. The second group was to receive special treatment, including rest in sick bays or heated barracks under doctors' care. The fate of the third group was not specified, but requires little imagination to picture. At the end of the month the OKW decreed that all prisoners in the Reich receive rations for working prisoners, supplemented by a week of gruel.

Only now, with winter weather closing in, did the military begin to change its prisoner transport policies as well – at least nominally. In November, Army Group Center stopped marching its prisoners to the rear on foot. On the twenty-second of that month, a senior officer in that army group's POW administration ordered that prisoners no longer be transported in open rail cars, because 20 per cent of the last transport from Bobruisk to Minsk – one thousand prisoners – had died. Still, only on 26 November did the army group order a thoroughgoing change to rail transport policies, and even after that point, transports in open cars did not cease. Many units at or near the front simply wanted to get rid of their prisoners, no matter what the consequences. In many cases between 25 and 70 per cent of prisoners died during transport, from a combination of exposure, hunger, and thirst. At the beginning of December the OKW's prisoner-of-war office decreed improvements in transportation, but the decree had little real effect.

The truth of the matter was that even after recognizing the prisoners' value as a source of labor, the German authorities were still not willing to care for them properly. At a conference on 7 November, Göring released guidelines for the prisoners' employment, in which he stated, 'The Russian is undemanding, and therefore can be fed easily and without serious inroads into our food balance. He should not be spoiled or get used to German fare, but must be fed such that his working ability is maintained to a level commensurate with the work he is required to do.'[12] One of the other attendees recorded Göring's further musings to the effect that a separate food supply should be created, in part from horses and cats, and that the prisoners' housing could be somewhat better than in their homeland, where many people lived in holes in the ground. Likewise, at the Orsha conference Wagner stated baldly that 'nonworking prisoners of war have to starve. Working prisoners of war can, in individual cases, be fed from army supplies. In view of the general food supply situation, unfortunately that cannot be ordered generally.'[13] And on the twenty-ninth, in a meeting at the food ministry, officials including General Reinecke and State Secretary Backe discussed the kinds of food that could be provided, including a so-called Russian bread consisting of 50 per cent rye meal, 20 per cent sugar beet mulch (left over from processing the beets), 20 per cent cellulose meal, and 10 per cent straw or leaves.

Even such food would only help if it reached the prisoners, and this was the point on which the supposed increases in rations broke down. By now the prisoner supply system had collapsed almost completely. The army would not provide more food, and the countryside could not. The influx of prisoners after the battles of Kiev, Vyazma, and Bryansk – more than 1.3 million of them, according to German figures – would have created problems, even under the best of circumstances. With the German logistical system straining to support the continuing offensive and, more important, given the uncaring attitude on the part of the senior leadership, the prisoners were doomed. The housing situation, moreover, was no better. The camps were last on everyone's list of priorities. As a result, for instance, by 1 November there were still over eighty-four thousand prisoners in so-called summer camps in occupied Poland, that is, without any shelter at all. As for the winter camps, they consisted of large, unheated halls in which the prisoners slept on bare floors, often without blankets. In the Reich, the OKH only planned for barracks for those prisoners it thought would improve enough to work, and many were never built in any case.

The results of these policies were predictably catastrophic. To cite just a few examples: Between 21 October and 30 October, 45,690 prisoners died in the camps in occupied Poland, an average of nearly 4,600 per day. In November, another eighty-three thousand died, 38.2 per cent of those present at the beginning of the month. By the end of November the death rates in the camps in the rear of Army Group Center had climbed to 2 per cent per day, and the rate increased further with the arrival of really cold weather. On

22 October, six hundred prisoners from the Wietzendorf camp in Germany were sent to Bremen to work, but the city administration could barely get any work out of them, and by 8 December half of them had died. By 1 December, Wehrmacht figures indicate that of five hundred thousand prisoners who had been sent to Germany, only three hundred fifty thousand remained, a 30 per cent loss in five months, and that in an area in which food supplies were plentiful. In all, by the beginning of December approximately 1.4 million Soviet soldiers had died in German captivity.

Suffering in the Civilian Sphere

When it came to caring for civilians in the occupied territories, the Germans were hardly better than they were with their prisoners. Nor were they more willing to accept their responsibility. Halder confided to his diary in early November: 'The northern wing [of Army Group South] is slowly advancing through the Donets basin, which the enemy has evacuated; the scorched-earth policy has been widely applied here, and the population probably will soon be faced with a serious food problem.'[14] Could Halder have believed that the population would not face a food problem if the Soviets had left everything intact? If so, he was seriously out of touch with reality. Beyond that, one detects a hint of petulance over the Soviet regime's unwillingness to surrender quietly, as expected.

Relatively few studies have documented the plight of Soviet civilians under German occupation in detail, but we do have an analysis of policies and practices in the area of General von Küchler's Eighteenth Army, in Army Group North. By October von Küchler's forces held a broad swath of territory south of Leningrad. Approximately three hundred fifty thousand civilians lived within that area, mostly women, children, and old men. This was not an agricultural region; dense evergreen forests and swamps dominate it, and the growing season is short. The population there needed food imports in order to survive, but this was part of the zone from which the Germans intended to withhold food for the sake of the army and the Reich. The regime's food policy faced several obstacles, however. First, there were conflicting priorities. While the food authorities at home insisted that food be withheld, the local economic offices complained that they would not be able to extract any labor from the population if it did not receive any food. Moreover, withholding food was bound to heighten security problems; the population was unlikely to submit quietly to the prospect of enforced starvation. And finally, withholding food was a morale problem for the army, and that morale problem translated into practical difficulties. For all the propaganda, and despite widespread faith in their cause, many German soldiers could not stand by and let women, children, and old people starve in front of their eyes without being affected, and without doing something about it. At the corps headquarters level, which actually had to deal with the civilians, the commands were pleading for food to give them, while some soldiers did what they could to alleviate the locals' suffering.

The higher commands reacted to these obstacles by stubbornly supporting the original food policy. On 3 November von Küchler's headquarters received word from Wagner: 'Every supply train from the homeland cuts back on foodstuffs there. It is better that our people have something and the Russians starve.'[15] He forbade the army command to feed civilians. Three days later von Küchler ordered that the troops be separated from civilians as much as possible, for reasons of 'security.' And he reminded the soldiers that local civilians 'belong to a racially foreign, hostile sort.'[16] (This was not a new argument on von Küchler's part; he had made similar statements before the campaign even opened.) The next day, 7 November, he and his principal staff officers agreed upon a new policy: they would literally make the problem go away. In the weeks that followed, Eighteenth Army drove tens of thousands of starving civilians out of its combat zone, into more remote areas that the German army did not physically occupy. The civilians who lived in those areas were already short of food. The results were obvious to anyone who cared to consider them.

At the conference in Orsha, Wagner reinforced his stand. Speaking now of the entire country, he said, 'The population can only be allowed the minimum for existence. In this regard the countryside will remain in a rather tolerable position. On the other hand, the question of feeding the larger cities remains unsolvable. There can be no doubt that especially Leningrad will have to starve, because it is impossible to feed that city. The leadership's task is to keep the troops away from that and from the associated manifestations.'[17] The struggle would continue at the lower levels, as some soldiers gave what food they could to local civilians in defiance of orders. At times they were giving away what their comrades had taken from other civilians during foraging expeditions. In the end, many more civilians would survive than the German leaders had expected; faced with starvation, Soviet citizens did what they could to find food. But hundreds of thousands, perhaps millions – no one knows for certain – would succumb in the harsh winter months.

The War against the Jews

By this time the effort to eradicate the Jews of the Soviet Union was in full swing. The killing squads continued, and even accelerated, their murderous activities through the autumn. Some, especially subunits of the *Einsatzgruppen*, followed along in the wake of the advancing combat troops, as they had always done. They found, however, that the numbers of Jews falling into their grasp was decreasing. One reason for this was geographic: the Germans had already advanced past the areas in which the greatest concentrations of Jews had lived. Another reason was that many Jews had left, some because they had heard about the Germans' intentions and others as part of the mass evacuations of workers, which the Soviets organized. According to some estimates, up to 1.5 million Jews escaped the German net. Be that as it may, the pace of the killing still increased, as other parts of the *Einsatzgruppen*, along with Order Police, Waffen-SS, army security divisions, military police, and local auxiliaries continued to attack the masses of Jews who still remained within the vast territories that the Wehrmacht had already overrun.

Again, there is no way to provide a comprehensive account of the killing squads' activities for the entire period. Instead, let us look at the month of October alone, and concentrate on the actions of the *Einsatzgruppen*, for which we have at least partial records. In the northern sector, *Einsatzgruppe* A reported that many Jews had fled eastward, but that it, together with local auxiliaries, had apprehended and concentrated the remaining Jews, and had killed or was killing all the men over sixteen years old, except for doctors and community elders. The report offered no numbers for those killed. We do know, however, that on 4 October the Germans began eliminating the people in the Wilna ghetto. The operation continued through 25 November and killed 12,388 people, not including Poles and prisoners of war. In addition, in Kaunas on 29 October the Germans shot 9,200 Jews whom they had designated as 'superfluous.'

In the region that the Germans called Weissruthenia – known more generally as Belorussia – *Einsatzgruppe* B's report indicates at least eleven different shootings, for a total of more than 3,600 victims. Here, in one concentrated dose, one finds a representative collection of the justifications and euphemisms that the killing units used in describing their victims and their supposed crimes; although in the Nazis' eyes the Jews' real crime was being Jewish, the killers could not come out and say so, apparently. They referred to 'Jewish Communists,' 'Jewish terrorists,' 'Jewish saboteurs,' and 'Jewish plunderers.' They accused the Jews of 'especially rebellious conduct,' 'spreading hate and cruelty propaganda about German occupation troops,' 'mounting resistance during the establishment of a ghetto,' and 'refusal to work.'[18] The report added that the *Einsatzgruppe* had begun with the elimination of three thousand Jews in the ghetto in Vitebsk, because of the danger of an epidemic. (In reality that danger came from the fact that the occupying authorities had not allowed any food into the ghetto; thousands there had already died of starvation.) The *Einsatzgruppe*, together with a battalion of Order Police, also killed another seven thousand Jews in the Mogilev ghetto on 2–3 and 19 October. Fewer than one thousand of the inhabitants remained alive to be placed in a forced labor camp. Another seven to eight thousand Jews in Polotsk and seven thousand Jews in Borisov were also killed. To those figures one can also add over 1,500 mental patients that the *Einsatzgruppe* killed in improvised gas chambers in Mogilev.

In the Ukraine, in addition to mentioning the shootings at Babi Yar the previous month, *Einsatzgruppe* C reported killing 3,145 Jews in Zhitomir, 'because experience shows that they had to be considered carriers of Bolshevik propaganda and sabotage.'[19] A further 410 Jews were killed in Cherson, supposedly in retribution for acts of sabotage. The report, which also included *Einsatzgruppe* D's operations, mentioned the liquidation of 4,891 Jews in the region east of the Dnieper – and actually we know that the figure only covers the first half of the month. According to postwar investigations, one subunit of *Einsatzgruppe* D alone killed approximately 12,500 Jews in four southern cities in October.

One should bear in mind, again, that the *Einsatzgruppen* were not the only units engaged in killing. Other murder squads, for example, killed ten to twelve thousand Jews on 12 October in the city of Stanislau, in Galicia. The next day, Higher SS and Police Leader Jeckeln had an Order Police battalion shoot approximately eleven thousand Jews in Dnepropetrovsk. Including those figures, even this incomplete accounting brings the number killed in October to over ninety thousand, most of them Jews, and not including prisoners of war or civilians whom the army eliminated.

Some historians argue that this was the period in which the Nazi regime decided on the so-called Final Solution of the Jewish question, that is, the physical extermination of all the Jews of Europe. The debate on the exact timing of that decision continues, and in fact it was probably not a single, sudden decision but rather a gradual process that involved both direction from above and initiative from below. By autumn several key steps had already taken place. One, of course, was the unleashing of the killing units. Another was the deportation of the first trainloads of Jews from Germany and other parts of Europe to the east. On 2 October Hitler had told Heydrich to rid the Reich of Jews by the end of the year; this meant that room would have to be made for them. In early November the SS announced it would ship fifty thousand German and Czech Jews to Riga and Minsk. In preparation, in the first half of November the SS and Police Leader in Minsk used Order Police and Lithuanian and Belorussian auxiliaries to kill about twenty thousand local Jews, in order to free up space for the German newcomers. Likewise, on 30 November and 8 December the Order Police, the staff of the Higher SS and Police Leader in Riga, and Latvian auxiliaries cleared out the Riga ghetto: they killed 26,000 Jews, leaving only 4,700 alive. On 30 November the first thousand German Jews reached Riga, where they were murdered immediately. More had frozen to death in the unheated rail cars during the journey. A week later at least another eight thousand were killed. Beside the fact of the killings themselves, one should note the timing: this was a period during which the Wehrmacht needed every trainload of supplies it could get, and yet trains were set aside to bring Jews to the east. Not only is this an indication of the Germans' priorities, but it also widens the circle of those who must have known that something was going on, since the General Staff took part in railroad scheduling. (In fact, the army did successfully protest the diversion of rolling stock after these transports went through.)

The Army's Role

The increased tempo of the killings continued to receive support from the army's leaders, for the same mix of practical and ideological reasons that had been present from the start. Security units were having an increasingly difficult time maintaining control, due to several factors. First, the Germans had overrun an enormous amount of territory. The Army Group Center rear area alone, for example, covered approximately fifty-six thousand square miles. To control it, the rear area commander had two infantry divisions, three security divisions, and an SS cavalry brigade at the beginning of October, in addition to SS and police formations and local auxiliaries, but that was not nearly enough. The civilians throughout the occupied lands were growing more restless, for reasons that the earlier description of their plight makes obvious. Partisan activity, while still disorganized, was picking up, while some security units were being sent to the front to help with the crisis there. The army reacted to the growing threat by cracking down even harder than it had before, if such was possible. The Jews continued to be the target of first choice, and the army's senior leaders made every effort to ensure that their men understood what was going on. General von Reichenau, for example, issued this order on 10 October, less than two weeks after the massacre at Babi Yar:

> The most important goal of the campaign against the Jewish–Bolshevik system is the complete crushing of the instruments of power and the eradication of the Asiatic influence in the European cultural sphere.
>
> In this connection there also exist tasks for the troops that extend beyond the traditional one-dimensional soldierly identity. In the east the soldier is not only a fighter according to the rules of warfare, but also the carrier of an inexorable racial idea and the avenger of all the bestialities that were inflicted upon the German and related races.
>
> Therefore the soldier must have full understanding for the necessity of harsh but just punishment of the Jewish sub-humans. It has the broader objective of nipping in the bud any uprisings in the Wehrmacht's rear, which experience shows to have always been instigated by Jews.

Only by applying the harshest measures, he continued, could the Wehrmacht 'free the German people from the *Asiatic-Jewish dan-*

ger once and for all.'[20] The order proved to be quite popular. Von Rundstedt liked it so much that he passed it on to the other two armies under his command as well as to the commander of his rear area. Hitler also got a copy, declared it to be outstanding, and ordered that it be sent to every unit on the eastern front. The recipients often added their own personal touches to the order before sending it to the troops. General von Manstein, for example, stated in his version that 'the Jews form the middle man between the enemy in the rear, the remainders of the Red Army that are still fighting, and the red leadership. . . . The Jewish-Bolshevik system must be eradicated once and for all. Never again may it intrude upon our European living space.'[21] And General Hoth, who had taken over command of Seventeenth Army, emphasized on 17 November that 'in this summer it has become ever clearer to us that, here in the east, inwardly irreconcilable world views are fighting. . . . We understand our mission clearly, to save European culture from the advance of Asiatic barbarism. . . . This battle can only end with the annihilation of one side or the other.'[22]

Von Reichenau also issued another order on 9 November, after a partisan attack that killed a regimental commander. This order provided concrete guidance on the battle against partisans:

> All captured partisans of either sex, in uniform or civilian clothes, are to be hanged in public. Any resistance attending their capture or transport is to be broken with the harshest means.
>
> All villages and farmsteads in which partisans are housed or cared for are to be called to account through the requisition of all foodstuffs, burning of houses, shooting of hostages and hanging of the guilty, when it cannot be indisputably established that the population defended itself against the partisans and suffered losses thereby.[23]

The indications are that the Wehrmacht was implementing orders such as these fully, with the aid of the *Einsatzgruppen*, the Order Police, the Waffen-SS, and local auxiliaries. On 3 November, *Einsatzgruppe*

C reported that it had an 'excellent understanding' with the military leadership in its sector, and Halder heard at the Orsha conference that the *Einsatzgruppen* were 'worth gold' to the fighting troops, because they secured the lines of communication to the rear.[24] Then there is the evidence of the killings themselves, of which a few examples will suffice. On October 29 the local army headquarters in Mariupol reported the killing of eight thousand Jews, whose apartments the headquarters staff took over. The local command shared out Jews' clothes and linens among the nearby military hospital, a prisoner-of-war camp, and ethnic German civilians. Less than two weeks later the Wehrmacht commander in Belorussia reported shooting 10,431 prisoners out of 10,940 taken in 'battles with partisans' in the previous month – but on the German side the losses amounted to two killed and five wounded, an impossible ratio for actual combat operations. And although the absolute numbers in this case were much higher than most, the ratios of Soviet to German casualties, and of Soviets captured to killed, were often much the same. Moreover, one should note this item in the commander's report: '2. Jews: . . . Because they are still making common cause with the Communists and partisans, the complete eradication of these foreign elements is being carried out.'[25] Farther north the story was the same; *Einsatzgruppe* A reported that the Wehrmacht in that sector had shot nineteen thousand Jews by December, and army units also continued to work with the killing units by transporting prisoners and cordoning off shooting sites. In the far south, Germany's allies demonstrated that they were willing executioners as well. After a bomb destroyed a Romanian military headquarters in the recently captured city of Odessa on 22 October, the Romanians killed thirty-nine thousand Jews and put another thirty-five thousand into two ghettos; fifteen thousand of the latter group died of neglect in the next three months.

As a counterpoint to all this, one should remember that the reality on the ground was complicated. Not all German soldiers were comfortable with the nature of the war, either as their commanders were defining it, or as they – the troops – saw it being prosecuted. The eastern army was huge, and even with the amount of indoctrination to which the soldiers were exposed, there were bound to be differences of opinion. The orders that von Reichenau and the other senior commanders issued to justify the killing are illuminating: if everyone had been acting according to the plan, there would have been no need to explain anything. Senior commanders in any army rarely explain matters of policy to the troops, after all. There is also evidence that even some senior officers were not prepared to toe the party line. One corps commander – General Eberhard von Mackensen – disseminated a very different kind of order than the one von Reichenau wrote. Von Mackensen enjoined his troops not to exploit the local population, but to treat them properly in order to win their support. Unfortunately he was a rare exception at that level. Lower down, however, there were some units that continued to hand Red Army stragglers, partisans, and suspects over to the *Einsatzgruppen*, or place them in POW camps, rather than shoot them themselves. Such behavior elicited an order from the XLIV Corps headquarters in November: 'Often, out of reasons of humanity or because the troops do not want to dirty their hands as executioners, the treatment of partisans that corresponds to their characteristics and their danger is rejected. . . . It is wrong to cultivate a noble attitude at the cost of German soldiers' lives.'[26]

Certainly there was an awareness at all the levels of command that, for all the propaganda, there was something wrong with the conduct of the campaign in the east. The troops must have noticed that, alongside the orders that justified the shootings, the command hierarchy also took steps to keep them secret. At roughly the same time that von Reichenau was issuing his order concerning the 'harsh but just punishment of the Jewish sub-humans,' other commands were enjoining their soldiers to stop taking pictures of shootings and sending them home, while still other directives aimed to keep the shootings out of sight of the troops entirely. There was also the matter of language. German orders were often masterpieces of euphemism; the reports, as we have seen, were collections of half-truths and dissimulation. No one in the command structure was in any doubt about what was going on, but they hesitated to put it in writing – and that fact betrayed their awareness that they were acting outside of commonly accepted moral and legal norms. Still, though, they continued to carry on, whether out of conviction or resignation, with the campaign of terror they had begun.

6

Failure and its Consequences, to Early 1942

When one examines the Germans' position at the beginning of December 1941, the phrase 'out on a limb' comes to mind. They had stretched their forces to the limit. They now occupied a front that stretched over 1,100 miles – roughly the straight-line distance from Boston to Jacksonville, Florida – and they held parts of that front only weakly. The weather was abysmal, with deep snows and subzero temperatures. Supplies were not getting through in sufficient quantities. Losses had been heavy, both from enemy action and from the cold. There were no reserves to speak of. The troops were growing dispirited. Despite its losses, the Red Army was still fighting, and the Soviet regime had not collapsed, contrary to German expectations. Clearly the campaign would continue into 1942, and in the meantime the army needed to rest and refit. It would not get the opportunity. On 5 December the Soviets launched a major counteroffensive against Army Group Center; soon the attacks would widen to include the other army groups as well. The Wehrmacht's leaders, who had assumed that they could retire to winter defenses without feeling too much pressure from their foes, now faced a potential catastrophe. Moreover, the war was about to broaden, with Germany's declaration of war against the United States. The

Germans' situation was taking a very different turn, and not for the better. They would react, in part, with new levels of barbarity, as they applied themselves to their long-term goal of solving the 'Jewish question.'

The Soviet Counter-Offensive Begins

This was the situation at the start of the month, in more detail (see maps 6 and 7). In Army Group North's area, Eighteenth Army's units were still tied down in front of Leningrad and along the coast to the west. Sixteenth Army had stretched out its line as far as Tikhvin while still holding a long section of front south from Lake Ilmen. Tikhvin was under constant Soviet attack, and von Leeb was preparing to abandon the town and take up a position farther to the southwest. At the other end of the front, von Kleist's First Armored Army, having been thrown out of Rostov, was continuing its retreat to the Mius River. Sixth and Seventeenth armies carried out some local attacks farther north in order to straighten their lines and then prepared to go on the defensive so that they could rest and refit.

In the center, the offensive against Moscow had all but come to a stop. On the northern wing the Soviets had fought Ninth Army and Armored Groups 3 and 4 to a standstill. The loss of the single bridgehead on the east side of the Moscow-Volga Canal extinguished the last hope for outflanking Moscow to the north. Fourth Army, directly in front of Moscow, had barely moved since the offensive reopened in November, due to continuing Soviet pressure and supply problems. Second Armored Army was still trying to take Tula, but without success; the Soviets were hanging on for dear life, as Guderian fought his army to the brink of exhaustion. At the southern end of the sector, Second Army was unable either to support Guderian's attack or to maintain contact with Army Group South. On 1 December it stopped its attacks and began digging in.

Von Bock and his staff knew that their forces now had to prepare to spend winter out in the open, but they had placed themselves in an impossible position. The decision to continue the offensive to the bitter end had led to a bitter end indeed. The attack had stalled, but virtually no preparations had been made for the defensive phase to come. The forward units were often in positions that were not suited for defense, and there were also no positions behind them. Nor could any be built, since both manpower and materials were lacking. All available forces had been thrown into the attack, leaving no units to build defenses, and supply priority had gone to fuel and ammunition for the offensive, and so the necessary construction materials had not been brought forward. Nor, for that matter, had winter clothing. The Germans' only ray of hope was the belief that the Soviets surely could not mount a major attack.

So much greater must have been the shock, then, as the Red Army struck Army Group Center with renewed ferocity in the early morning hours of 5 December. At that point the Soviet forces facing von Bock numbered approximately 1.1 million troops, with more than 7,600 guns and nearly eight hundred tanks. At points along the attack front they managed to create a two-to-one advantage in men, a slightly lesser superiority in artillery, and near parity in armored vehicles – and all of it without arousing German suspicions. The attack came in temperatures of five degrees Fahrenheit, with more than three feet of snow on the ground. On the German side, any thought of rest for the troops had to be discarded immediately. Now the fight was to survive.

The Soviets directed their main attacks at several different points, with the initial aim of cutting off the German spearheads on either side of Moscow. Ninth Army and Armored Groups 3 and 4 faced attacks against Kalinin and Klin on the northern flank, from the area around Dmitrov on the Moscow-Volga Canal, and farther south toward Istra. Against Guderian's Second Armored Army, the Soviets trapped the units at the tip of the bulge around Venev and attacked out of the Tula salient. The Germans shifted forces laterally in a desperate effort to shore up the front and buy time for withdrawals. Guderian immediately began to pull his units back toward the Don River, southeast of Tula, where he hoped to form a coherent defense. The Soviets lacked the strength and the experience to take full advantage of their gains – many of their units had been badly mauled during the defensive battles of the previous weeks – and so their efforts to encircle and destroy whole German armies failed. They did make many local penetrations, however, and did serious damage to several German divisions and one corps in the process. Soviet forces also began to infiltrate deep into the German rear and attack headquarters and supply points. A series of increasingly panicked messages began to filter up through the Wehrmacht's command system.

The seriousness of the situation at the front took some time to make itself felt at the top, apparently. Halder's diary reveals no special sense of urgency for the first few days after the Soviet offensive began. On 8 December, Hitler issued orders for the continuation of operations in the east; von Brauchitsch followed up the same day with a more detailed order for the army. Hitler's directive stated that because of a surprisingly early winter and the resulting supply difficulties, the army would go onto the defensive immediately. The goal for the winter months would be to rest and refit, while denying operationally and economically important areas to the enemy. The army would be allowed to make limited, local withdrawals to better defensive positions, but only after those positions were ready. Army Group North should complete the encirclement of Leningrad and link up with the Finns. Army Group South was to take Sevastopol and, if possible, to establish a bridgehead over the Don near Rostov during the winter, in preparation for an offensive into the Caucasus in the spring. As for Army Group Center, von Brauchitsch's order stated that 'after the conclusion of the operation against Moscow,' the army group was to organize its forces for defensive operations.[1]

One can only wonder what 'conclusion' von Brauchitsch had in mind; the order does not specify. He can hardly have believed that

major offensive operations were still possible. In fact, even the orders
for a defensive operation were out of date when they were issued.
At the front, army commanders were already starting to withdraw
their forces on their own authority, under heavy enemy pressure. In
some areas those efforts to retreat failed: the snows were deep, trucks
and tanks were breaking down in the cold, fuel was running out, and
the army's few remaining horses were at the end of their strength.
The same problems plagued efforts to counterattack. Everywhere
the front seemed in danger of disintegrating. Von Bock told Halder
on 8 December that his army group was unable to repel Soviet
attacks at any point along the front. Guderian was considering further withdrawals. General Rudolf Schmidt, commander of Second
Army, feared a major Soviet breakthrough that would cut the railroad
between Orel and Kursk, thus splitting his forces and disrupting the
flow of supplies. North of Moscow the Soviets had reached Klin and
were approaching Solnechnogorsk on 9 December, having advanced
nearly twenty miles in some areas. All the German generals began
shouting for reinforcements, but few were to be had, especially in the
short term. Fresh units from Germany or the western theaters would
not arrive for weeks. The only immediately available men were in
the security and supply units, and their removal from the rear areas
meant that desperately needed supplies fell prey to partisan attacks or
sat at the supply depots.

The Germans now faced an impossible choice: to hold in place
or to withdraw. The former option entailed the possibility of being
bypassed, surrounded, and destroyed piecemeal. The latter meant losing virtually all the heavy equipment, since there was no way to
transport it, and in addition the lack of positions in the rear meant
that the troops were likely to find themselves worse off in the end.
The OKH had designated a provisional line to which Army Group
Center could retreat, but von Bock and von Kluge concluded on 10
December that they would either have to fight in place or pull back
well beyond the OKH's line – and von Bock was not ready to order
such a retreat on his own responsibility, since his armies would lose

so much equipment in the process. By December 12 Halder, replacing complacency with hyperbole, was speaking of 'the worst crisis in the two world wars.'[2] Von Bock and his subordinates, reacting in disbelief to the orders that Hitler and von Brauchitsch released on 8 December, now demanded that von Brauchitsch visit the front personally. They could only conclude that their reports were not reaching him unaltered. When he arrived at von Bock's headquarters on 13 December, they pressed for a general withdrawal. Von Brauchitsch replied that he was aware of the troops' condition and agreed with the need for a pullback. He and the others were now thinking of a retreat to the line from Kursk through Orel, Kaluga, and Gzhatsk to Rzhev.

A period of heightened confusion and conflict now set in within the German command system. The generals wanted to retreat. Hitler, on the other hand, continued to insist that a retreat made no sense if, at the end of it, the troops found themselves in the open with no heavy weapons. On 14 December he gave his permission for local withdrawals by Ninth Army and Armored Groups 3 and 4, but nothing more, while he also pushed von Bock to accelerate the preparation of new defensive positions along the line from Kursk to Rzhev. Two days later Halder explained to von Bock that even the approved withdrawals were only to be carried out as a last resort. Guderian, whom von Bock had put in charge of Second Army and Second Armored Army together, was to cut off Soviet penetrations north of Livny and west of Tula, and then hold the line from Livny to Aleksin. Fourth Army, whose front had remained stable and which had thus been able to build up some defenses, was to hold in place. In the meantime Hitler was directing that forces from Germany and the west be rushed to the front as quickly as possible. Von Bock doubted that they would get through in time, and in a conversation with Hitler's adjutant on the night of 16 December he held out little hope that the army group could hold either in its current positions or farther to the rear. He obviously had no solutions to offer; for the most part he seems to have been intent on getting someone else to accept responsibility for the mess into which he had helped place his command.

On 18 December the Soviets opened a second phase of their offensive, with attacks against von Bock's central sector. The next day Halder's first diary entry for Army Group Center read simply, 'Attacks everywhere.' By evening he knew of new breakthroughs in three places. 'Situation very tense,' he wrote.[3] The Fourth Army chief of staff informed him that the troops were becoming apathetic, that the Russians attacked by night and were behind the forward positions by daybreak. There was little Halder could do, however, except offer encouragement; the OKH was already working as hard as it could to get reinforcements and replacements to the front. Certainly Hitler's attitude was showing no sign of change; on 20 December he reiterated his demands that the army hold and fight to the last, that it not take one step back voluntarily, that enemy breakthroughs were to be eliminated. The goal was to win time for the arrival of reinforcements. In the meantime, though, gloom was spreading through the command; Jodl even compared the army's plight with Napoleon's in 1812.

Jodl made that remark in a briefing with von Leeb, who had come to Hitler's headquarters to discuss the situation in the north. His forces, like those facing Moscow, had been under intense Soviet pressure. On 5 December the Red Army had surrounded Tikhvin in temperatures reaching thirty degrees below zero. Hitler had ordered von Leeb to hold the town until relief arrived, but relented to an evacuation two days later. Von Leeb's plan at that point was to pull Sixteenth Army back to an intermediate position east of the Volkhov River. By 16 December, however, Soviet attacks forced a further retreat. Von Leeb went to the Führer's headquarters to obtain approval for that withdrawal – although in fact he had already ordered it. Hitler relented, with the caveat that the Volkhov was to be held to the last man. Von Leeb could only hope that the Soviets would not be able to concentrate significant forces for an attack on Sixteenth Army's new line, where thirteen infantry and two armored divisions, exhausted and short of equipment and supplies, held a front more than 120 miles long. In any case, hopes of isolating Leningrad or linking up with the Finns had disappeared completely; the army group's objective for the campaign was impossible to meet.

In the south, the main action was taking place in the Crimea, where von Manstein's Eleventh Army was preparing to attack the Soviets' last stronghold, the port of Sevastopol. The German bombardment opened on 13 December, but the attack had to be postponed twice because of a lack of air support. On the seventeenth it finally went forward and made good initial progress, though with heavy losses. The attack had to be halted again, however, on 26 December, when the Soviets landed forces on the Kerch Peninsula at the eastern side of the Crimea. Hitler and von Reichenau demanded that Sevastopol be taken and the Kerch cleared at the same time, although von Manstein's army clearly could not perform both missions simultaneously. On 31 December, having paid lip service to the Führer's wishes, von Manstein suspended the assault on Sevastopol in order to deal with the Soviet forces in the Kerch.

The War Widens

While the Germans fought with increasing desperation on the eastern front, the war's horizons were changing dramatically. On 7 December, Japan attacked the United States, and Hitler declared war on America four days later. People have wondered about his decision ever since, but in truth, Hitler had believed for years that he would have to fight the United States sooner or later. He knew that his navy was too weak to take on the Americans directly, but with Japan on his side, that point seemed moot. Most of the Wehrmacht's leaders shared his opinion that taking on the Americans did not represent a great risk militarily. As subscribers to the 'stab in the back' myth, most of them did not believe that the United States had contributed much to Germany's defeat in the First World War, and so they easily dismissed America's potential. The commander in chief of the navy, Admiral Erich Raeder, was positively itching for a fight, while the army and the air force paid hardly any attention to this new development at all. Halder, who still occasionally took time to make note of international developments in his diary, had nothing whatsoever to say on the German declaration. Whether because he was too wrapped up in the crisis in the east or because he had all but given up on strategic thinking, he failed to comment on the event that all but sealed the Third Reich's fate.

The first appraisal of this new development's significance came from the OKW. On 14 December it released a document entitled 'Overview of the significance of the entry of the U.S.A. and Japan into the war.' Despite some errors, the document's analysis of the enemy situation was remarkably accurate. It stated that Japan's entry and its initial successes had thrown the Allies' strategic plans out the window, and that the Allies could not regain any kind of strategic initiative until autumn 1942 at the earliest. Beyond that point they would have three options: to concentrate on Europe and the Atlantic, to concentrate against Japan, or to hold and stabilize on all fronts until they had built up their strength. For planning purposes the staff assumed that the Allies would choose the first and, for Germany, the worst course. Decisive operations under that option would not be possible in 1942, since the United States would not have mobilized fully, the staff supposed, and after that the greatest threat would be to northwest Africa or Norway. (The Allies would invade North Africa in November.) The OKW then went on to draw conclusions for the coming year's operations, and here it proved less astute. It suggested that Germany would be able to bring its operations in the east to a successful close in 1942 by cutting off the ports of Murmansk and Archangel (through which the western Allies were shipping war material) and by taking the oil region of the Caucasus. Those gains would allow Germany to hold off its enemies for the foreseeable future, and in addition the Caucasus would make an excellent jumping-off point for operations into the Near East.

Hitler's analysis of the situation was similar in many respects. He was determined to continue the campaign in Russia, and the Caucasus oil fields had long been one of his targets. Up until late in 1941 he had wanted to press forward along the entire front, but the Soviet counteroffensive persuaded him that the Wehrmacht would not have the strength for that. Both manpower and equipment were lacking, the latter especially because Hitler had shifted production priorities to the air force and navy in July, in anticipation of a rapid victory; he would reverse that decision in the coming January, but months would pass before the effects would become apparent. Therefore he decided to make the main thrust in the south, toward the Caucasus and Stalingrad. He still believed that Britain might give up if its position became hopeless, and further that a German victory in Russia, combined with Japanese gains in the Far East, might bring the British around. As far as the United States was concerned, Hitler had no idea how to defeat it, but he covered his uncertainty with bluff and bluster. Beneath it all he had come to recognize that the war was going to last for years and, without expressing it clearly, he had decided on a defensive, continental strategy, at least for the time being.

Changes in Command

The crisis on the ground was something new for the Wehrmacht, and it produced a corresponding crisis in command. Von Brauchitsch was the chief victim. His position had become more and more difficult over the course of the campaign. Above him stood the Führer, insisting that he knew how to run a campaign better than anyone else. As Hitler said at the end of October, 'I am the field commander against my will; I only concern myself at all with military things because at the moment there is no one who could do it better.'[4] Any reverse, perceived failure, or hesitation was enough to bring the supreme commander's wrath down upon his subordinate. In the meantime, von Brauchitsch also had to face Halder and the other generals. He frequently agreed with their opinions, but he was powerless to affect Hitler's actions, and few of those below him were slow to recognize that fact. On 31 July Halder wrote, 'The commander in chief is unfortunately unable to arrange to place even a hint of his own will in [one of Hitler's orders]. It is dictated out of the concern that it suggest no contradiction of those above.'[5] The strain told on von Brauchitsch increasingly as the campaign wore on. On 10 November Halder recorded that his commander had suffered a heart attack the night before, but von Brauchitsch continued to work from his hospital bed, and less than three weeks later he was back on duty. The arrival of the December crisis brought matters to a head, however. Halder noted: 'The commander in chief is hardly even a messenger boy anymore. The Führer goes over his head to the army group commanders.'[6] On 15 December he wrote that von Brauchitsch was 'very depressed and sees no way to save the army from its difficult situation.'[7] On 19 December Hitler finally relieved him, at his own request. 'I'm going home,' von Brauchitsch told Keitel, 'He has relieved me; I can't do any more.'[8]

Hitler did not name another general to take over in von Brauchitsch's stead, but rather took over immediately himself. He saw the chance to blame the emerging debacle in the east on von Brauchitsch and the OKH (as well as on the other commanders), while he could appear as the savior of the situation. He also had political goals in mind. Halder reported him as saying, 'Anyone can handle the little task of directing operations. The task of the commander in chief of the army is to train the army in a National Socialist sense. I do not know a general in the army who can fulfill this task as I wish. Therefore I have decided to take over command of the army myself.'[9] The army's reaction to Hitler's move is illuminating. After the war, many officers referred back to this moment as marking the death of the army's independence and the final step in the rise of the amateur Hitler. At the time, however, few expressed such misgivings. On the contrary, Hitler's takeover appeared to be the perfect solution to the army's problems. Now the army's needs and priorities might receive more attention. Even Halder did his best to accommodate himself to the new arrangement, in the hope that he could work with Hitler more successfully than von Brauchitsch had.

After he told Halder of his decision, and of his wish that Halder stay on as chief of the General Staff, Hitler proceeded to lecture him in typical style. Two mistakes had been made up to this point, he said. The first was that the term 'rearward position' had been allowed to take hold among the troops. Such positions were not available and could not be created. The second mistake was that not enough preparations had been made for the winter. As far as the front was concerned, the thing to do was to hold, without fear of threats on the flanks. That evening Halder gathered his staff officers together to inform them of the change. There is no record of his exact remarks, but the attitude seems to have been that von Brauchitsch had reached the end of his endurance, and that the army would benefit by having Hitler at the helm. A few days later Halder would write to the senior commanders that 'we can and should be proud that the Führer himself is now at the head of our army.'[10]

Von Brauchitsch was not the only one to lose his position during the crisis. In fact, a wholesale shake-up in the army's senior ranks was already underway. Von Rundstedt had gone first, after the retreat from Rostov began. Von Bock was next; he went the day before von Brauchitsch. He had sent word to Hitler late on 16 December that his health was hanging 'by a silken thread' and that if the Führer believed that a fresh mind was needed, he should not hesitate out of consideration for him (von Bock). On the evening of the eighteenth, von Brauchitsch relayed Hitler's message to von Bock that the latter should request a leave of absence to regain his health. (This avoided the appearance that von Bock was being relieved for having failed, and indeed Hitler would later give him another army group command.) Von Kluge took over command of the army group.

Guderian went next. He had an independent streak that strained his relationships with his superiors. In recent weeks he had twice given his army orders to retreat without waiting for permission to do so; on other occasions he had rejected operational instructions from Halder and von Bock. He had gone over the heads of his immediate superiors, as well as Halder and von Brauchitsch, and appealed to Hitler directly, through Hitler's adjutant. Finally on 20 December he flew to the Führer's headquarters to meet with him face-to-face. The two men met for nearly five hours that evening, with only a couple of interruptions. Guderian told Hitler about the conditions at the front and about his plans for a pullback. Hitler immediately forbade such a move. Guderian told him it was already under way. (He would maintain later that von Brauchitsch had approved the withdrawal six days earlier, and that he was amazed that Hitler did not know that.) They argued back and forth – Halder later described the discussion as 'dramatic' – but the Führer would not budge. The problem was that determination alone would not stop the Soviets. Over the following days Guderian kept insisting that he be allowed to run his army as he saw fit. When the conflicts between Hitler and Guderian (with von Kluge caught in the middle) became too great, Guderian finally requested to be relieved of his command, and Hitler obliged him. General Schmidt took over.

Hoepner, commander of Armored Group 4, departed later under similar circumstances, as did Field Marshal von Leeb. Hoepner, on his own authority, ordered a corps to break out of a Soviet encirclement on 8 January, 1942. Hitler sacked him, and demanded that he lose his pension and his right to wear the uniform. (Someone actually had the temerity to tell Hitler that such measures were impossible without a court martial. Later he had the Reichstag grant him the authority to deal with similar situations as he saw fit.) On 15 January, von Leeb insisted that he either be relieved or given freedom of action; Hitler chose the former.

On 21 December Halder had assured the chief of staff of Army Group Center that if everyone could just hold on for another fourteen days the whole thing would be over, that the enemy could not possibly keep up his frontal attacks much longer. Instead, by early January the Soviets had broadened their offensive. No longer did they simply want to blunt the German attack on Moscow. On 7 January Stalin ordered a general offensive along the entire front, despite his generals' recommendations that he concentrate his strength. Already the Red Army had taken Kalinin and Kaluga, and they were besieging a series of cities throughout the central and northern sectors, many of them well behind the front line, inasmuch as one even existed. By trying to advance everywhere, however, Stalin robbed his units in the center of the strength they needed to eliminate the German forces there. The attacks continued on through the winter, but with the spring thaw the Soviets finally had to give up. The German lines looked more like a half-finished jigsaw puzzle by that time, and losses had been horrendous. Even by the following May the General Staff would estimate that the eastern army was still short 625,000 men, mostly in combat units. The material situation was no better. As of 20 March 1942, the army had suffered net losses of over 115,000 transport vehicles, 3,100 armored vehicles, 10,400 artillery pieces, and 160,000 horses. The Luftwaffe had nearly six hundred fewer aircraft than at the start of the campaign and, amazingly, forty fewer than in September 1939. Still, the Soviets had missed the opportunity to inflict truly catastrophic losses on Army Group Center, and though weakened, the Wehrmacht would be able to reconstitute itself for an offensive in 1942.

Behind the Lines

Winter is hard on soldiers. The creature comforts of civilian life are available only in diluted form, or not at all. The cold, the wet, and the gray skies can produce a level of apathy and misery that most of us never have to experience, if we are lucky. Winter in Russia takes that discomfort to extremes. Even fit, relatively well-fed and well-clothed young men find that their minds go numb along with their extremities. Fingers and toes, sometimes feet and hands, are lost. Sometimes the loss is more general: the brain gradually goes into a kind of daze, and the body drifts off into death. For prisoners of war and civilians, stripped of clothing and shelter, fed little or nothing for weeks before winter even set in, their bodies already weak, the suffering is indescribable, the end often predictable. Such was the situation in the winter of 1941–1942, which marked one of the greatest periods of mass mortality in history. The German army, having already demonstrated, at the very least, its lack of concern for the people of the occupied territories, and caught up in its own crisis, paid scant attention as the policies of the previous months bore horrible fruit.

Some Soviet prisoners of war continued to fall victim to the *Einsatzgruppen*, which now had free access to all camps. The reports that the *Einsatzgruppen* sent back to Berlin in December and January detail a succession of such shootings. 'In the course of a thorough examination in the prisoner-of-war camp in Vitebsk,' *Einsatzgruppe* B reported on 22 December, '207 prisoners were apprehended and shot.' The group performed similar duty in the POW camp in Vyazma, where '117 Jews were caught and shot.'[11] By this time, however, the program was winding down; soon the authorities would suspend it entirely. One reason was that the Germans were capturing fewer prisoners as their advance faltered. Another was that the failure of the campaign and the need for labor made the surviving POWs more valuable. In any case, the toll had already grown to enormous proportions: although we will never have an exact figure, the best estimate is that the Germans shot up to half a million Soviet prisoners. The SS itself estimated that 10 to 20 per cent of the POWs were selected for execution – and the Germans captured approximately 3.35 million Soviet soldiers in the first six months of the campaign.

For most of the remaining prisoners, the policy changes that the authorities enacted in November and early December, in an effort to increase their captives' capacity for work, came too late, to the extent that they were implemented at all. Within the zone of operations the crisis at the front drew away what little attention the army had been willing to spare for its prisoners to begin with. The Wehrmacht simply did not make food available, and the country-side could not provide more. The camps were lucky to get rations at the old levels. In Gulag 240 in Rzhev, for example, the prisoners received an average of 1,435 calories per day in December. Twenty-two per cent of them died between 24 November and 15 December, a period of three weeks. In the rear the conditions were hardly bet-ter; as at the front, lack of food and housing, inadequate medical care, and improper transport combined with the onset of true win-ter weather to kill off further thousands of the already weakened prisoners.

Efforts to alleviate the prisoners' plight were minimal. On 3 December, Armaments Minister Fritz Todt assumed responsibil-ity for those prisoners who were to work as skilled laborers in the armaments industry. He ordered adequate food and care, and made housing for thirty thousand prisoners available. By then, however, many prisoners were beyond help. Ministerialdirektor Werner Mansfeld, head of the labor allocation group in the office of the Four-Year Plan, recorded that 29.4 per cent of the POWs in the *Reichskommissariat* Ostland – sixty-eight thousand men – died in December, an average of 2,190 per day. In the Ukraine the figure was 46.4 per cent, for a total of 134,000, or 4,300 per day. The death rate in those territories declined somewhat in January, but still remained high. In the General Government, sixty-five thousand prison-ers died in December. That was a lower absolute number than in November, but it represented 45.8 per cent of those present at the beginning of the month; in November the figure had been 38.2 per cent. In the Reich the total was 72,000 out of 390,000 POWs: a lower per centage than in the General Government, but higher than in the area of operations, where supply difficulties were presumably greater.

To give an overview of the POWs' plight in statistical terms: On average, about six thousand Soviet prisoners died every day between the start of the campaign and the end of January 1942 – and that does not include those whom the Germans shot. Overall, over two million of the Red Army soldiers who fell into German hands in 1941 were dead by 1 February of the following year: more than 65 per cent. Of those who were left, few were in any condition to work.

Soviet civilians were often hardly better off. In Leningrad, for example, the German blockade had put nearly three million people at risk for starvation – just as the Wehrmacht intended. Air raids had destroyed significant stocks of grain, flour, and sugar. The Soviets set up a supply line across Lake Ladoga, first by boat and later across an ice road, but conditions were extremely primitive and the amount of food that the boats and trucks could bring in came nowhere near to meeting the city's needs. The authorities cut rations five times before December, by which time people had already begun to die of hunger and disease. In 11 November,000 died; in December, 52,000; in January, between 3,500 and 4,000 per day. Eventually the toll would reach into the hundreds of thousands, perhaps more than a million; no one knows the exact total.

Conditions were similar in the territories that the Germans actually controlled. The army was still collecting much of what food it could find, leaving many of the local civilians with little or nothing to get them through the winter. Moreover, additional deprivations were in the offing. On 21 December Hitler released a 'summary of the tasks for the army for the immediate future.' In this order, which included the operational instructions that Hitler had issued to Halder the day before, he also inserted two casually vicious directives: 'Prisoners and residents to be stripped of their winter clothing ruthlessly' and 'All surrendered farmsteads to be burned down.'[12] In the Russian winter, such orders amounted to nothing less than death sentences. Hitler also called for the exploitation of civilian, POW, and concentration camp labor to make up for the millions of German soldiers who would not be returning to the home front. How many died as a result of these policies, no one can say, but the numbers were certainly high, given the perilous circumstances in which so many civilians already lived.

Policies would begin to change somewhat over the course of 1942, but a fundamental conflict would arise between two sides in a policy debate. The prolongation of the war meant that Germany's need for raw materials, food, and labor was all the greater, and there were those who favored maximum exploitation, in accordance with the Nazi ideology that had dominated so far. On the other side were those (a distinct minority) who wanted to try to gain the active help of the local populations, for reasons both pragmatic and humane. On the pragmatic side, they saw that stripping civilians of all they possessed would only generate resistance; others simply rejected the idea that Slavs should be treated like animals. Over the course of time an imperfect compromise emerged, as the Germans tried to implement both strategies in a sort of carrot-and-stick approach. The incentives they were prepared to offer, however, were minimal, while their arrogance and brutality never faded. There was never any realistic attempt to appeal to people's political or economic aspirations, never any real promise of freedom or land reform. The authorities did ease off on food requisitions in 1942, but they also started rounding up civilians by the tens and then hundreds of thousands for use as forced laborers, both in the occupied east and in Germany. When all is said and done, perhaps the Germans could have turned the peoples of the occupied east into their allies in 1942, but the question is moot, because the required policies were never under consideration to any meaningful extent.

Among the civilians in the occupied east, disappointed, hungry, and deprived of all their rights, open hostility toward the Germans became more and more prevalent. That sentiment, of course, fed directly into the partisan movement. The *Einsatzgruppen* report for December notes that the occupying authorities had expected the partisan threat to slacken as winter weather took hold, but in fact

they found the opposite to be true. The partisans were still strug-
gling to establish themselves, and they devoted much of their effort
to building up base areas and procuring food for the winter, but
they also continued – and in some areas, increased – the tempo of
their active operations. They blew up bridges and rail lines, attacked
German convoys, gathered intelligence for the Red Army, interfered
with food shipments into the cities, and assassinated local officials.
The Germans, meanwhile, were unable to fight the partisans as effectively as they had before. Not only did the winter weather restrict
movement through the countryside, but although the *Einsatzgruppen*
continued to operate in the rear, the crisis at the front called many
SS, police, and Wehrmacht security units to combat duty. Behind the
front, the Germans tried to make use of every available force, including reserve regiments, training units, and officers' and NCOs' classes,
for the antipartisan war. All they could do, however, was guard supply
routes and key points; any active pursuit of the partisans was out of
the question. The *Einsatzgruppen* reports reflected the same state of
affairs: they made much of a few victories, but the small scale of the
operations was impossible to hide.

From this point forward the partisan movement would be a constantly growing threat to the German war effort, while the Germans'
antipartisan campaigns suffered from a lack of manpower as well as
from internecine squabbling over authority. Preemptive brutality
continued to be the preferred method for fighting the guerrillas,
although over time the dominant doctrine shifted from mass executions to mass deportations – even if the former practice never
disappeared completely – the idea being to starve the partisans of
support while feeding labor into German industry. Neither tech-
nique was successful, from the Germans' standpoint: all they did was
drive more recruits into the partisan bands and increase the level of
support that the rest of the population provided.

The Fate of the Jews

The Germans continued to justify the extermination of the Jews in the Soviet Union by citing the need to fight the partisan movement. Himmler's diary entry for 18 December, which records a meeting with Hitler, contains the line 'Jewish question / to be exterminated as partisans.'[13] The note obviously represented confirmation from the Führer, rather than a new policy direction; the equation Jew = Communist = partisan had been in force from the start of the campaign. The *Einsatzgruppen* reports, even while they said little about direct operations against partisan units, continued to draw the connection in describing actions against the Jews. The report for December cited a 'special action' in Bobruisk, in which they shot 5,281 Jews, in part for maintaining contacts with partisans, as well as for refusing to wear their markings, refusing to work, and displaying a provocative attitude toward the occupying troops. With that action, the report continued, the city and region of Bobruisk were free of Jews. Likewise, the report stated that partisans in the area around Gomel were receiving support from Jews, so another 2,365 Jews were shot there. Similar actions took place in Rudnja, near Smolensk (835 killed); in Paritschi, near Bobruisk (1,113); in Rovno (15,000); and in Vitebsk, where the SS cleared the ghetto (4,090). The report for January stated, without a trace of irony, that 'the attitude of the Jews is, as before, clearly hostile to Germans, and criminal.'[14]

As the winter deepened, some killing units reduced the pace of their operations, in part for much the same reasons that the antipartisan campaign slowed: bad weather, reduced mobility, and the crisis at the front, which drew some army and SS units into combat. The *Einsatzgruppen* and some other police units remained active, however. The area directly behind the armies was yielding even fewer victims than before: not only had most of the few Jews in that area fled or been killed, but the stalled offensive meant that no new victims were being overrun. The Soviets even saved some from villages they liberated in their counteroffensive. The other side of the coin, though, was that the slowness of the advance also gave the killing units time in which to fulfill their mission more completely, as well as to backtrack and begin a second, more thorough sweep of areas already covered. The goal of the second sweep was to exterminate all the remaining Jews in the Soviet Union, with the exception of skilled workers in some larger ghettos. Entire populations of smaller, more remote cities and towns, as well as significant proportions of Jews living in the larger ghettos, fell victim in this second round of killing, which would last through 1942. By the time it was over, the *Einsatzgruppen*, Order Police, Waffen-SS, and army units, together with Germany's allies and local auxiliaries, had shot a total of roughly 1.5 million people – mostly Jews, but also suspected Communists, partisans, prisoners of war, and people with mental and physical disabilities.

The army remained fully informed of the *Einsatzgruppen* activities and continued to play its part in the killing, even as the Soviet counteroffensive gained strength. On 14 December, for instance, following long discussions between the Wehrmacht and a subunit of *Einsatzgruppe* C, the military commander in Kharkov ordered all Jews to gather. On the sixteenth the Germans confined approximately fifteen thousand Jews inside a tractor plant, where they held them for ten days. Between 26 December and the middle of the following month, the SS and Police Battalion 314 shot most of the Jews; the remainder were murdered in one of the now-operational gas vans. Farther south, Eleventh Army headquarters ordered the Secret Field Police and the *Abwehr* – the Wehrmacht's counterintelligence branch – to hand over Jews to *Einsatzgruppe* C. Local field commanders and military police also joined in an operation that wiped out nearly all the Jews in the Crimea by spring 1942, with help from local militia, agents, and tips from the region's inhabitants. Ten thousand Jews died in Simferopol alone. Moreover, neither the winter weather nor the Soviet counteroffensive prevented some army units from continuing the 'Jew hunts' in the rear areas, as in the zone behind Army Group Center, where soldiers killed 2,200 Jews in February, mostly in the countryside.

The Final Solution and *Barbarossa*

For much of the summer and autumn, Hitler and his subordinates had been working toward a decision regarding the 'Jewish question.' There is still debate among historians over the timing of the decision and the process by which the Nazis reached it. There was, as far as we know, never any written order to exterminate the Jews of Europe. The fact of the decision is not in question, but it probably evolved over time, in a process that involved a certain amount of give-and-take among Hitler, Himmler, and other key leaders in Berlin and in the field. We can safely say that the decision was firm by the end of November at the latest, although there are certainly indications that Hitler was thinking about extermination much earlier. At any rate, by mid-autumn the Nazis' plan to deport the Jews to Siberia or Madagascar had fallen by the wayside. The indefinite prolongation of the campaign in the Soviet Union meant that the territories of the eastern Soviet Union would not be available any time soon, and Britain's continued control of the sea precluded shipping the Jews to the distant French colony. The killing units' operations had revealed limitations – shooting was too slow, too public, and too hard on the perpetrators – but they had also opened the Nazis' minds to the possibility of exterminating all the Jews of Europe. This was to be the so-called Final Solution.

Hitler expounded upon the new policy at a meeting with the Nazi Party's regional leaders on 12 December. Josef Goebbels, the propaganda minister, recorded the Führer's thoughts in his diary:

> Concerning the Jewish question, the Führer is determined to make a clean sweep. He prophesied to the Jews that if they were once again to cause a world war, the result would be their own destruction. That was no figure of speech. The world war is here, the destruction of the Jews must be the inevitable consequence. This question is to be viewed without sentimentality. It is our duty to have sympathy not for the Jews but only for our own German people. If the German

people have now again sacrificed 160,000 dead on the eastern front, then the authors of this bloody conflict must pay for it with their lives.[15]

On 29 November Heydrich had sent out invitations for a conference on Jewish policy, to be held on 9 December in the Berlin suburb of Wannsee. The outbreak of war with the United States forced a delay, but on 20 January, 1942, Heydrich and other representatives of the SS met with senior figures from the Eastern, Interior, and Justice ministries, the Four-Year Plan, the Foreign Office, the Reich Chancellery, and the General Government. The purpose of the meeting was not to make new decisions, but to establish clear lines of authority and begin working out the details of implementation. Heydrich succeeded in establishing himself as the man in charge of the program; all the other agencies would have to follow his lead. In his main address he spoke in euphemisms, but a frank discussion of killing methods followed. The target, as Heydrich explained, was to be the approximately eleven million Jews in the region stretching from Portugal to the Ural Mountains and from Ireland to the Middle East. Later he expressed his satisfaction at the apparent enthusiasm of all concerned.

At the time of the Wannsee conference, the Nazi leaders still were not certain how the practical aspects of the killing were going to work; that is, they were not sure how well the techniques then available were going to handle the tremendous numbers of victims involved. In the field, however, the necessary solutions were under development. By the end of the year, several gas vans had been constructed, and all four of the *Einsatzgruppen* were using them. In addition, extermination camps were either planned or under construction at Auschwitz/Birkenau, Sobibor, and Belzec, and the camp at Chelmno had been in operation since 8 December. Further gassing facilities at Treblinka and Lublin/Majdanek would open later in 1942. The killing centers would transform murder into an efficient, industrialized process, as the statistics indicate: At the beginning of

1942, only 25 per cent of those who would ultimately die in the Holocaust were already dead; by the end of the year, that figure would reach 75 per cent.

The end of 1941 saw the Germans' hopes for quick victory against the USSR disappointed. In the north, although Leningrad was under siege, the Wehrmacht had succeeded neither in capturing nor in isolating it. The birthplace of the Bolshevik Revolution would suffer terribly in the coming years, but it would not fall. In the south, the Germans had penetrated nearly 750 miles into Soviet territory, capturing valuable industry and resources in the process – but they had not achieved the goal of destroying the Soviet forces in the region. And in the center, Moscow had also held fast. Overall, even though the Wehrmacht had dealt the Soviets a series of incredibly heavy blows, neither the Red Army nor the Soviet government had collapsed. With that fact, the entire premise of the campaign had proved a chimera. Now the Germans were stuck. They would not be able to mount an offensive of the same scale the following year, and even though they would seem to have the Soviets on the ropes once again, in the end their efforts would lead them to Stalingrad and their greatest defeat to date.

The Germans were also fixed upon occupation policies that were morally reprehensible, illegal, and counterproductive. Having entered into the campaign with the expectation that it would be short and triumphant, and with a belief in their own racial and ideological superiority, the Wehrmacht's leaders saw no need for leniency toward the conquered peoples. They gave free rein to their soldiers' most brutal impulses, and in fact encouraged them to commit murder. The result was an increasing level of resistance and the disappearance of opportunities for any real economic gain. Also, word of the Germans' excesses inevitably made its way across the lines and bolstered Soviet determination to fight to the death.

Here, then, at the end of 1941, was the culmination of German goals and policies in the east: an army stuck in the snows, fighting for its life; behind it, an occupation regime of exploitation and murder; in front of it, an enemy growing more implacable by the day. Few Germans understood the links among those three aspects of their situation, and none of them was in a position to do much about it.

Conclusion

The German invasion of the Soviet Union in 1941 is instructive on at least two levels. First, it highlights the combination of ruthlessness and prejudice that informed German military strategy and occupation policy. And second, it demonstrates how interconnected ideology, culture, politics, economics, and warfare can be.

What drove Nazi Germany to invade the USSR and to implement policies there that violated every civilized norm? At the deepest level, one must look to the interaction of many influences, some of which reach back at least to the nineteenth century, such as a culture that emphasized German superiority within a competitive, racist world view, along with particular antipathy toward Slavs, and religious and political antisemitism. Other influences arose out of the experience of the First World War and its aftermath, such as radical anti-Marxism (and the conflation of Marxism with Jewishness), as well as the belief that the survival of the German people depended upon another war, and that such a war would demand total commitment at home and the unrestricted use of force against the enemy. None of these factors made the outcome inevitable; even in combination, they could not have forced Germany down a particular path. But they do help us to understand the path it took.

In a more immediate sense, a collection of strategic and ideological reasons contributed to the decision to attack the Soviet Union. Victory over France had given the Germans an inflated faith in their own military prowess, but had not provided an easy way out of their strategic dilemma. Britain was still in the fight, and there was no simple way to defeat it. With other options lacking, Hitler turned his attention eastward, thinking that if he conquered the Soviet Union, Britain would lose a potential ally and perhaps see the hopelessness of its situation. Such a strategy came easily to Hitler's mind, of course, because he had always wanted to conquer additional territory in the east; he believed that Germany's survival depended upon acquiring that Lebensraum. Moreover, conquest in the east would give Germany the food and raw materials it would need to win the fight against Britain and, ultimately, the United States. And, last but certainly not least, Hitler was determined to destroy the 'Jewish-Bolshevik' state, the center, he believed, of the greatest threat to western civilization since the Mongols.

Hitler's generals supported his decision, in part because they shared his goals, and in part because they also shared his confidence in an easy victory. The Soviet state had purged its military of most of its senior commanders and had demonstrated its military incapacity against opponents as unimpressive as the Finns and the Poles. Furthermore, the generals believed that Nazi Germany, in addition to its innate racial and political superiority, possessed the finest military in the world; after all, they had just defeated the French in a matter of weeks. Surely the Wehrmacht would have no problem defeating the Red Army west of the Dvina/Dnieper line, after which the corrupt political structure of Stalinist Russia would simply collapse. The campaign would be over by early September, by the very latest, and the Wehrmacht could then turn its attention back to the pesky British, leaving a token force in the east to control the Reich's new empire there.

In order to ensure their victory, the generals also helped lay the plans for Hitler's vision of an exterminationist war. Later they would claim that the SS was solely responsible for the crimes in the east, but in fact the military's role was crucial. At the most basic level, the crimes could never have taken place if the Wehrmacht had not conquered the ground, but the generals' culpability extends well beyond that fact. They encouraged their soldiers in an attitude that placed little or no value on the life of Soviet civilians; in fact they ordered their men to use the harshest conceivable means to establish German dominance. They planned for the deliberate starvation of millions of people and for forced labor by millions more. They laid the groundwork for the fatal neglect of Soviet prisoners of war, whose care was their responsibility by international law. And they played a key role in planning for the elimination of the Communist leadership and intelligentsia, including those in uniform, as well as anyone who resisted German rule. That last goal provided the perfect cover for the SS *Einsatzgruppen* and other killing units to murder anyone whom they saw as a threat, including hundreds of thousands of Jewish men, women, and children. Since most of the military's leaders believed that Jews were fundamentally hostile and dangerous, they were able to persuade themselves, with little apparent difficulty, that killing all the Jews was necessary to secure the conquered territories.

Once the military operations got under way on 22 June, the Germans' faith in their abilities seemed justified. Surprise was nearly total, and within days the Wehrmacht had penetrated the border defenses and was racing deep into the rear, disrupting communications, dislocating Soviet attempts to regroup, taking key positions, and killing or capturing hundreds of thousands of enemy troops. By early July German leaders were already proclaiming victory and planning for the postwar army. By the end of the month the German spearheads were already approaching Leningrad and Kiev, and in the center they had taken Smolensk. On the surface, everything seemed to be going according to plan.

Already, however, signs were emerging that the campaign was not proceeding so smoothly as the generals believed. True, their forces could move forward with confidence wherever they could concentrate, but they could not be strong everywhere. The Soviets were fighting back desperately; even though they had taken enormous losses, there was no sign of either a military or a political collapse. The demands on the Wehrmacht were outstripping its resources; for every threat it eliminated, another remained just out of reach. In addition, the Germans were also having to come to grips with the inadequacies of their logistical arrangements. Rates of consumption of fuel and ammunition were higher than expected, and the transport system simply could not deliver the volume of supplies that the armies required. So far none of these problems could threaten the German advance in any serious way, but the portents were not good.

This was the moment when the debate over the campaign's objectives came to a head. The generals wanted to strike at Moscow; they believed that the Soviets would throw their best remaining units into the fight for the capital, both because of its political significance and because it was an important transportation hub and industrial center. Hitler, on the other hand, had never believed that Moscow was that important: he wanted to capture Leningrad, thus freeing up the Baltic, and he also wanted the resource-rich territories of the Ukraine. He and his advisers argued for weeks, but in the end Hitler insisted on his plan and sent Army Group Center's mobile forces north and south. The result in the Ukraine was another great victory for German arms, and hundreds of thousands more prisoners.

Despite the scope of their triumph, however, the Germans still were not able to produce a Soviet collapse. Leningrad was holding out, the offensive in the south seemed to go on and on without result, there were significant Soviet forces in front of Moscow, and the Wehrmacht's logistical difficulties were only increasing. Now the Germans again turned their attention to the Russian capital, in the hope that with one more victory they could push the Soviets over the brink and win the campaign. The offensive began in early October, and again the initial progress was stunning. Once more the Germans rolled over whole Soviet armies and captured hundreds of thousands more prisoners. The way to Moscow appeared open. Then the rains came, and the Wehrmacht's advance slithered to a halt in the mud. When the ground froze in early November, mobility returned, but the cold created new problems, and the attack faltered. The Wehrmacht had reached the end of its strength; the last goal (as the generals perceived it) proved beyond its reach. The dream of victory in one campaign season was dead. Now it was the Soviets' turn: their counteroffensive took advantage of the Germans' vulnerability and came close to destroying them. Only Hitler's determination, Stalin's miscalculations, and the endurance of the Wehrmacht's soldiers saved the situation.

While the military campaign was going on, another facet of the war was developing in the lands that the Germans had overrun. The 'necessity of war' and Nazi ideology came together to produce a series of crimes the likes of which the modern world had never seen. Those few Germans who wanted to gain the willing cooperation of the peoples of the USSR fought a losing battle against those who saw greater benefit in brutality. The SS and the Wehrmacht executed hundreds of thousands: prisoners of war, suspected partisans, Communist functionaries, Jews, and people with disabilities. Millions more died of starvation, exposure, disease, and exhaustion, as the German army took their food, forced them to work, drove them from their homes, and sometimes even requisitioned their winter clothes. As their policies spawned resistance, the Germans reacted with still harsher repressive measures, which they directed first and foremost at the Jews. The war's prolongation eventually inspired some modifications to German occupation policy, but much too late to have any effect before spring 1942. Moreover, by then the killing units' success had opened the Nazis' minds to new, and ultimately 'final,' solutions to the problems inherent in their ideology.

At least two broad conclusions become apparent from an examination of Operation *Barbarossa* and the crimes that went along with it. On the purely military level, one can see that the Germans set themselves an overly ambitious goal and then, through poor planning and ruthlessness, made its achievement even less likely. The Soviet Union was not Poland, or even France. The scale of the theater, the inadequacy of the transportation network, and the severity of the climate were physical obstacles of no small note. Together with the strength of the Soviet regime (which the servants of another totalitarian state should perhaps have expected), the size of the Red Army, and the USSR's vast human and industrial resources, those obstacles should have produced more caution among German planners. The generals gambled that the Soviets would collapse, and doubtless their decision seemed more reasonable at the time than it does to us today. The generals' mistake, though, was that they failed to treat their decision as a gamble, and that failure led to others. First, the Germans had no fallback position, no alternative plan should the Soviets continue to fight. Given the Wehrmacht's lack of reserves in nearly every category of military supplies, equipment, and manpower, a bit more thought to contingencies would have been in order (although this also would have been a departure from German military practice stretching back into the nineteenth century: the Germans had always depended upon quick operational victories to secure strategic goals). Second, faith in quick victory also removed any incentive to take full advantage of the local population's hostility to the Soviet regime, even as a temporary measure. Granted, the imperatives of Nazi ideology probably would have prevented any real alliance, but the fact remains that the military's leaders never took such a course into consideration. The criminal orders and their implementation were another aspect of that same error. Many people in the Soviet Union had a hard time believing that anything could be worse than Stalin's dictatorship, but the Germans proved such a thing possible.

The other broad conclusion has to do with the relationship between the military and criminal aspects of *Barbarossa* and developments in the war as a whole. We can see, for one thing, that the events in the Soviet Union were a strong influence upon the decision for the so-called Final Solution of the Jewish question (or at least its European stage; the Nazis had plans for other regions too). On the one hand, the relative success with which the Nazis rounded up and shot hundreds of thousands of innocent people helped to convince Germany's leaders that extermination was a real option, while the prolongation of the war helped close out deportation as an alternative and encouraged a sense of urgency, a belief that the solution could not wait until after final victory. At the same time, the Germans could also see the limitations in the killing units' operations; their search for other methods led them to the gas chamber and the death camp. Returning to the military sphere, with the failure of Operation *Barbarossa* and the declaration of war against the United States, Germany needed a miracle to win, and such a miracle was not forthcoming. Stalingrad may have been the emotional turning point of the war, but the Germans' best chance for victory disappeared in the snows in front of Moscow, if not earlier. Given the Nazis' vision for the world, that is something for which we can only be thankful.

Maps

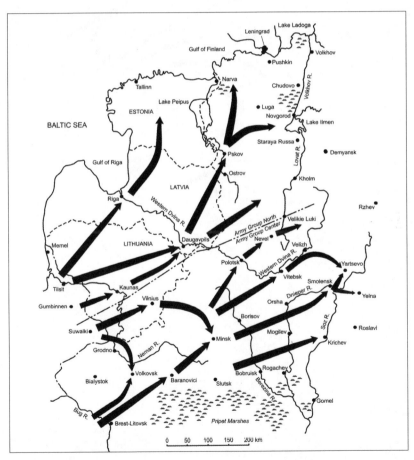

Map 1 Army Group North and Center, 22 June–ca. 31 July

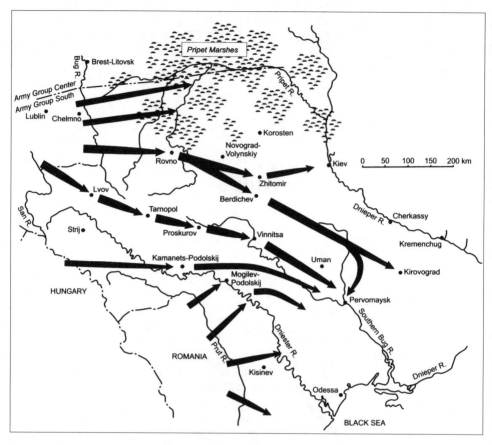

Map 2 Army Group South, 22 June–ca. 31 July

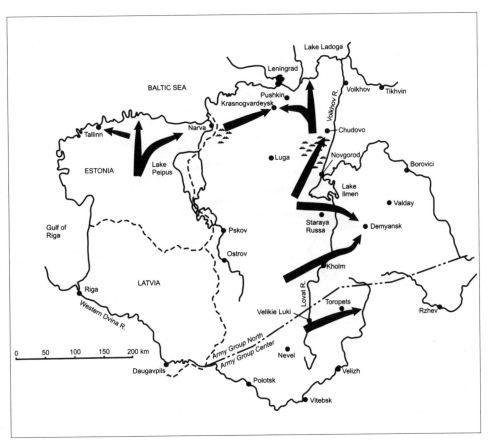

Map 3 Army Group North, ca. 1 August–1 September

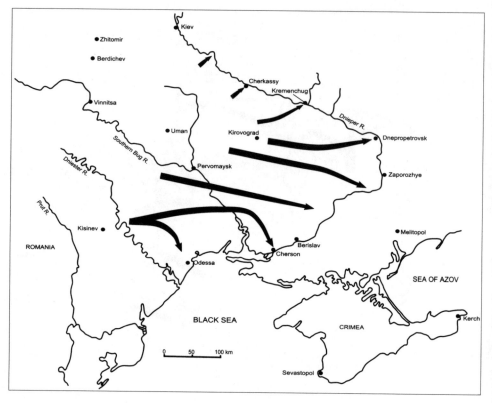

Map 4 Army Group South, ca. 1–25 August

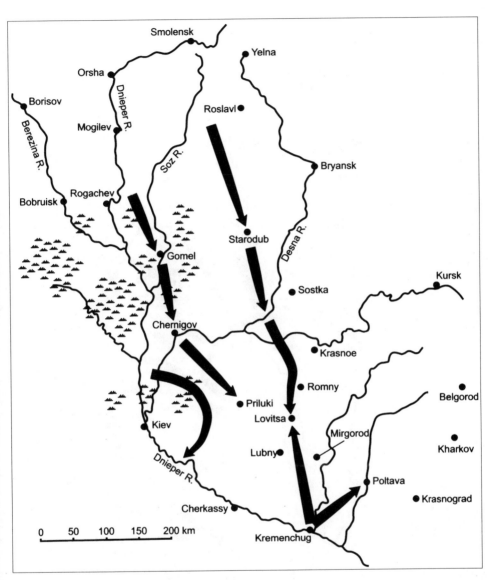

Map 5 Army Groups North and Center, ca. 1 October–5 December

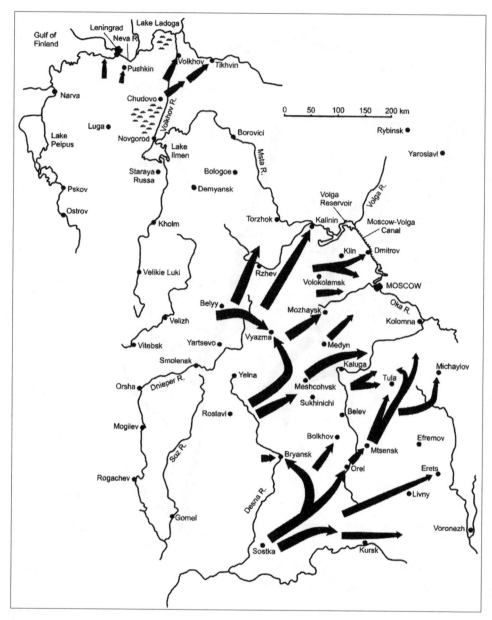

Map 6 Army Groups North and Center, ca. 1 October–5 December

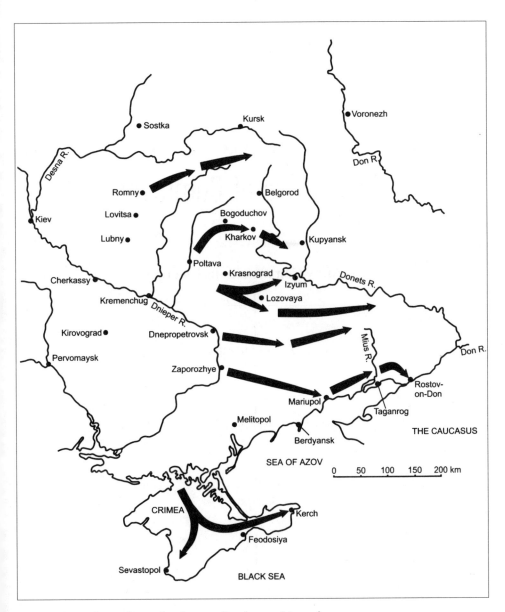

Map 7 Army Group South, ca. 1 October–25 November

The Levels of Command

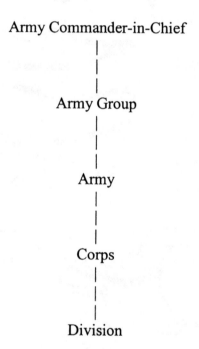

Army Commander-in-Chief

Army Group

Army

Corps

Division

Generally speaking, a division contains between ten and fifteen thousand men and is the smallest unit capable of independent operations, with its own supporting arms and supply organization. The levels above that consist of headquarters, each of which controls two or more of the elements below it. Thus a corps consists of two or more divisions, and so on.

Principal German Army Commands and Staffs on June 22, 1941

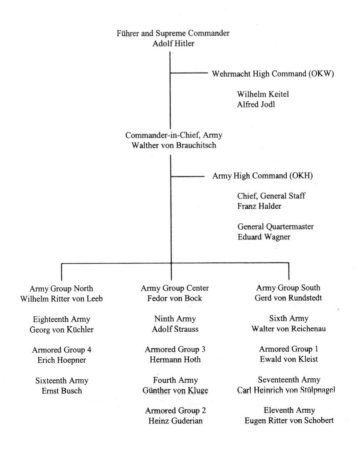

Führer and Supreme Commander
Adolf Hitler

Wehrmacht High Command (OKW)

Wilhelm Keitel
Alfred Jodl

Commander-in-Chief, Army
Walther von Brauchitsch

Army High Command (OKH)

Chief, General Staff
Franz Halder

General Quartermaster
Eduard Wagner

Army Group North	Army Group Center	Army Group South
Wilhelm Ritter von Leeb	Fedor von Bock	Gerd von Rundstedt
Eighteenth Army	Ninth Army	Sixth Army
Georg von Küchler	Adolf Strauss	Walter von Reichenau
Armored Group 4	Armored Group 3	Armored Group 1
Erich Hoepner	Hermann Hoth	Ewald von Kleist
Sixteenth Army	Fourth Army	Seventeenth Army
Ernst Busch	Günther von Kluge	Carl Heinrich von Stülpnagel
	Armored Group 2	Eleventh Army
	Heinz Guderian	Eugen Ritter von Schobert

Notes

CHAPTER 1: THE ROOTS OF THE WAR OF ANNIHILATION

1   Adolf Hitler, *Mein Kampf*, trans. Ralph Manheim (Boston: Houghton Mifflin, 1943, 1971), 654.

2   Quoted in Manfred Messerschmidt, 'Foreign Policy and Preparation for War,' in *Germany and the Second World War*, ed. Militärgeschichtliches Forschungsamt (Research Institute for Military History), vol. 1, *The Build-up of German Aggression* (Oxford: Clarendon, 1990), 544–45.

3   Quoted in Paul Heider, '*Der totale Krieg – seine Vorbereitung durch Reichswehr und Wehrmacht*,' in *Der Weg deutscher Eliten in den Zweiten Weltkrieg*, ed. Ludwig Nestler (Berlin: Akademie Verlag, 1990), 43–44.

4   Quoted in Thilo Vogelsang, '*Neue Dokumente zur Geschichte der Reichswehr, 1930–1933*,' *Vierteljahreshefte für Zeitgeschichte* 2 (1954): 432.

5   Vogelsang, '*Neue Dokumente*', 434.

6   Both quotes are from Jürgen Förster, 'Hitler's Decision in Favour of War Against the Soviet Union,' in *Germany and the Second World War*, ed. Militärgeschichtliches Forschungsamt (Research Institute for Military History), vol. 4, *The Attack on the Soviet Union* (Oxford: Clarendon, 1996), 34–35.

7   The quote comes from a speech that Hitler gave in Nuremberg, probably in September 1935; a film of the speech is on view at the United States Holocaust Memorial Museum in Washington.

8   Franz Halder, *The Halder War Diary, 1939–1942*, ed. Charles Burdick and Hans-Adolf Jacobsen (Novato, Calif.: Presidio, 1988), 346 (March 30, 1941).

9   Christian Hartmann and Sergij Slutsch, '*Franz Halder und die Kriegsvorber-eitungen im Frühjahr 1939: Eine Ansprache des Generalstabschefs des Heeres*', *Vierteljahreshefte für Zeitgeschichte* 2 (1997): 483. Readers should be aware that some scholars have questioned the authenticity of the record of that meeting. The sentiment, however, is authentic.

10   Quoted in Alexander Rossino, *Hitler Strikes Poland: Blitzkrieg, Ideology, and Atrocity* (Lawrence: University Press of Kansas, 2003), 13.

11   Quoted in Hans Umbreit, '*Auf dem Weg zur Kontinentalherrschaft*' in *Das Deutsche Reich und der Zweite Weltkrieg, vol. 5/1, Organisation und Mobilisierung des Deutschen Machtbereichs*, ed. Militärgeschichtliches Forschungsamt (Stuttgart: Deutsche Verlags-Anstalt, 1988), 29. One should note that some historians have cast doubt on the verity of this account of the meeting, especially regarding Hitler's statement on the killing of civilians.

12   Quoted in Rossino, *Hitler Strikes Poland*, 117.

CHAPTER 2: PLANS AND PREPARATIONS, 1940-1941

1   Walther Hubatsch, *Hitlers Weisungen für die Kriegführung 1939–1945: Dokumente des Oberkommandos der Wehrmacht* (Wolfenbüttel: Wolfenbütteler Verlagsanstalt, 1949), 96–97.

2   Franz Halder, '*Der Komplex OKH-OKW*,' in the Halder papers, BA-MA N 220/95, 36, 46–47.

3   Andreas Hilgruber, '*Noch einmal: Hitlers Wendung gegen die Sowjetunion 1940*,' *Geschichte in Wissenschaft und Unterricht 33* (1982): 220.

4   Quoted in Christian Streit, *Keine Kamaraden: Die Wehrmacht und die sowjetischen Kriegsgefangenen 1941–1945*, 2nd ed. (Bonn: Dietz, 1997), 62.

5   Jürgen Förster, 'Operation *Barbarossa* as a War of Conquest and Annihilation,' in *Germany and the Second World War*, ed. Militärgeschichtliches Forschungsamt (Research Institute for Military History), vol. 4, *The Attack on the Soviet Union* (Oxford: Clarendon, 1996), 485.

6   Quoted in Helmut Krausnick and Hans-Heinrich Wilhelm, *Die Truppe des Weltanschauungskrieges: die Einsatzgruppen der Sicherheitspolizei und des SD 1938–1942* (Stuttgart: Deutsche Verlags-Anstalt, 1981), 117.

7   To see photostatic copies of this and most other orders discussed here, see Hamburger Institut für Sozialforschung, ed., *Verbrechen der Wehrmacht: Dimensionen des Vernichtungskrieges 1941–1945; Ausstellungskatalog* (Hamburg: Hamburger Edition, 2002); the order quoted here is on pp. 58–59. For discussions of them in English, see Förster, 'Operation *Barbarossa* as a War of Conquest and Annihilation,' and also Theo J. Schulte, *The German Army and Nazi Policies in Occupied Russia* (Oxford: Berg, 1989).

8   Quoted in Förster, 'Operation Barbarossa as a War of Conquest and Annihilation,' 485–86.

9   Quoted in Jürgen Förster, 'Securing "Living-space"' in *Germany and the Second World War*, vol. 4, *The Attack on the Soviet Union*, 1194.

10   Quoted in Krausnick and Wilhelm, *Die Truppe des Weltanschauungskrieges*, 217.

11   The quote is from the order itself, which appears in Hamburger Institut für Sozialforschung, ed., *Verbrechen der Wehrmacht*, 52–53.

12   Förster, 'Operation *Barbarossa* as a War of Conquest and Annihilation,' 508.

CHAPTER 3: INITIAL VICTORIES AND ATROCITIES, JUNE TO AUGUST

1   Franz Halder, *The Halder War Diary, 1939–1942*, ed. Charles Burdick and Hans-Adolf Jacobsen (Novato, Calif.: Presidio, 1988), 446–47.

2   Walter Warlimont, *Inside Hitler's Headquarters*, trans. R. H. Barry (New York: Praeger, 1964), 180.

3   Halder, *Diary*, 424.

4   Halder, *Diary*, 432.

5   Halder, *Diary*, 448.

6   Percy Ernst Schramm, ed., *Kriegstagebuch des Oberkommandos der Wehrmacht*
    (*Wehrmachtführungsstab*) (Munich: Pawlak, 1982), 1:1019.
7   Wagner is quoted in Jürgen Förster, 'Securing "Living-space"' in *Germany and the Second
    World War*, ed. Militärgeschichtliches Forschungsamt (Research Institute for Military
    History), vol. 4, *The Attack on the Soviet Union* (Oxford: Clarendon, 1996), 1228.
8   Quoted in Christian Streit, *Keine Kamaraden: Die Wehrmacht und die sowjetischen
    Kriegsgefangenen 1941–1945*, 2nd ed. (Bonn: Dietz, 1997), 106; emphasis in original.
9   Quoted in Norbert Müller, Uwe Löbel, and Ulrich Freye, eds., *Die faschistische
    Okkupationspolitik in den zeitweilig besetzten Gebieten der Sowjetunion (1941–1944)* (Berlin:
    Deutscher Verlag der Wissenschaften, 1991), 161. See also Förster, 'Securing 'Living-space''
    1196–97.
10 Quoted in Förster, 'Securing 'Living-space'' 1197.
11 Quoted in Streit, *Keine Kamaraden*, 106.
12 Quoted in Helmut Krausnick and Hans-Heinrich Wilhelm, *Die Truppe des
    Weltanschauungskrieges: die Einsatzgruppen der Sicherheitspolizei und des SD 1938–1942*
    (Stuttgart: Deutsche Verlags-Anstalt, 1981), 219.
13 Order of July 2, 1941, quoted in Krausnick and Wilhelm, *Die Truppe des
    Weltanschauungskrieges*, 157.
14 Quotes from Krausnick and Wilhelm, *Die Truppe des Weltanschauungskrieges*, 163–64.
15 Quoted in Förster, 'Securing "Living-space"' 1204.

CHAPTER 4: THE SECOND PHASE: EXPANDING, CONQUESTS AND GENOCIDE, AUGUST TO OCTOBER

1   Percy Ernst Schramm, ed., *Kriegstagebuch des Oberkommandos der Wehrmacht
    (Wehrmachtführungsstab)* (Munich: Pawlak, 1982) (hereafter OKW KTB), 1:1061.
2   Franz Halder, *The Halder War Diary, 1939–1942*, ed. Charles Burdick and Hans-Adolf
    Jacobsen (Novato, Calif.: Presidio, 1988), 506.
3   Halder, *Diary*, 537.
4   OKW KTB, 1:1068; emphasis in original.
5   Quoted in Christian Gerlach, *Kalkulierte Morde: Die deutsche Wirtschafts- und
    Vernichtungspolitik in Weißrußland 1941 bis 1944* (Hamburg: Hamburger Edition, 1999), 604.
6   Quoted in Helmut Krausnick and Hans-Heinrich Wilhelm, *Die Truppe des
    Weltanschauungskrieges: die Einsatzgruppen der Sicherheitspolizei und des SD 1938–1942*
    (Stuttgart: Deutsche Verlags-Anstalt, 1981), 219.
7   Quoted in Krausnick and Wilhelm, *Die Truppe des Weltanschauungskrieges*, 208–9.
8   From Bock's diary, quoted in *Germany and the Second World War*, ed. Militärgeschichtliches
    Forschungsamt (Research Institute for Military History), vol. 4, *The Attack on the Soviet
    Union* (Oxford: Clarendon, 1996), 584 n192.

CHAPTER 5: THE FINAL DRIVE ON MOSCOW AND SYSTEMATIC KILLING, OCTOBER TO DECEMBER

1   Max Domarus, *Hitler: Reden und Proklamationen 1932–1945; Kommentiert von einem deutschen
    Zeitgenossen* (Wiesbaden: Löwit, 1973), 2:1757–58; emphasis in original.

2 Elizabeth Wagner, ed., *Der Generalquartiermeister: Briefe und Tagebuchaufzeichnungen des Generalquartiermeisters des Heeres, General der Artillerie Eduard Wagner* (Munich: Günter Olzog, 1963), 207.

3 Quoted in Ernst Klink, 'The Conduct of Operations: The Army and Navy,' in *Germany and the Second World War*, ed. Militärgeschichtliches Forschungsamt (Research Institute for Military History), vol. 4, *The Attack on the Soviet Union* (Oxford: Clarendon, 1996), 673–74.

4 Wagner, *Der Generalquartiermeister*, 210.

5 Here I have chosen to translate the original German, as more exact. Franz Halder, *Kriegstagebuch: Tägliche Aufzeichnungen des Chefs des Generalstabes des Heeres 1939–1942*, ed. Arbeitskries für Wehrforschung, Stuttgart (Stuttgart: Kohlhammer, 1962) (hereafter Halder KTB), 3:306 (Nov. 23, 1941); emphasis in the original. Halder made virtually the same remarks at both conferences.

6 Wagner, *Der Generalquartiermeister*, 289; Eckstein's personal record of the interchange is in the Wagner papers in the military archive in Freiburg, Germany: BA-MA N 510/27.

7. Franz Halder, *The Halder War Diary*, 1939–1942, ed. Charles Burdick and Hans-Adolf Jacobsen (Novato, Calif.: Presidio, 1988), 556.

8 Halder, *Diary*, 569.

9 Quoted in Helmut Krausnick and Hans-Heinrich Wilhelm, *Die Truppe des Weltanschauungskrieges: die Einsatzgruppen der Sicherheitspolizei und des SD 1938–1942* (Stuttgart: Deutsche Verlags-Anstalt, 1981), 254.

10 From von Bock's diary, Nov. 9, 1941, quoted in Krausnick and Wilhelm, *Die Truppe des Weltanschauungskrieges*, 254.

11 Quoted in Christian Streit, *Keine Kamaraden: Die Wehrmacht und die sowjetischen Kriegsgefangenen 1941–1945*, 2nd ed. (Bonn: Dietz, 1997), 145.

12 Quoted in Streit, *Keine Kamaraden*, 145.

13 Quoted in Streit, *Keine Kamaraden*, 157–58.

14 Halder, *Diary*, 551.

15 Quoted in Johannes Hürter, 'Die Wehrmacht vor Leningrad: Krieg und Besatzungspolitik der 18. Armee im Herbst und Winter 1941/42,' *Vierteljahrshefte für Zeitgeschichte 49/3* (July 2001): 409.

16 Quoted in Hürter, 'Die Wehrmacht vor Leningrad,' 414.

17 Quoted in Streit, *Keine Kamaraden*, 158.

18 Quoted in Peter Klein, ed., *Die Einsatzgruppen in der besetzten Sowjetunion 1941/42: Die Tätigkeits- und Lageberichte des Chefs der Sicherheitspolizei und des SD* (Berlin: Gedenk- und Bildungsstätte Haus der Wannsee-Konferenz, 1997), 230.

19 Quoted in Klein, ed., *Die Einsatzgruppen*, 232.

20 Quoted in Streit, *Keine Kamaraden*, 115; emphasis in von Reichenau's original order.

21 Quoted in Streit, *Keine Kamaraden*, 116.

22 Quoted in Klein, ed., *Die Einsatzgruppen*, 78.

23 Quoted in Krausnick and Wilhelm, *Die Truppe des Weltanschauungskrieges*, 264.

24 On Einsatzgruppe C's report, see Jürgen Förster, 'Securing "Living-space'in *Germany and the Second World War*, 4:1205 n83; on Halder at Orsha, see Krausnick and Wilhelm, *Die Truppe des Weltanschauungskrieges*, 267.

25 Krausnick and Wilhelm, *Die Truppe des Weltanschauungskrieges*, 274.

26 Krausnick and Wilhelm, *Die Truppe des Weltanschauungskrieges*, 267.

Notes

CHAPTER 6: FAILURE AND ITS CONSEQUENCES, TO EARLY 1942

1   Percy Ernst Schramm, ed., *Kriegstagebuch des Oberkommandos der Wehrmacht* (*Wehrmachtführungsstab*) (Munich: Pawlak, 1982) (hereafter OKW KTB), 1:1078.

2   Quoted in Earl F. Ziemke and Magna E. Bauer, *Moscow to Stalingrad: Decision in the East* (New York: Military Heritage Press, 1988), 78.

3   Franz Halder, *Kriegstagebuch: Tägliche Aufzeichnungen des Chefs des Generalstabes des Heeres 1939–1942*, ed. Arbeitskries für Wehrforschung, Stuttgart (Stuttgart: Kohlhammer, 1962) (hereafter Halder KTB), 3:355.

4   Werner Jochmann, ed., *Adolf Hitler: Monologe im Führerhauptquartier 1941–1944; Die Aufzeichnungen Heinrich Heims* (Munich: A. Knaus, 1982), 101 (night of 21–22 Oct., 1941).

5   Halder KTB, 3:136.

6   Halder KTB, 3:332.

7   Halder KTB, 3:348.

8   Walter Görlitz, *Generalfeldmarschall Keitel: Verbrecher oder Offizier? Erinnerungen, Briefe, Dokumente des Chefs OKW* (Göttingen: Musterschmidt-Verlag, 1961), 287.

9   Peter Bor, *Gespräche mit Halder* (Wiesbaden: Limes, 1950), 214. The words may not be accurate – Halder did not write them down until after the war – but the sentiment certainly fits.

10   Quoted in Ernst Klink, 'The Conduct of Operations: The Army and Navy,' in *Militärgeschichtliches Forschungsamt* (Research Institute for Military History), ed., *Germany and the Second World War*, vol. 4, *The Attack on the Soviet Union* (Oxford: Clarendon, 1996), 718.

11   Yitzhak Arad, Shmuel Krakowski, and Shmuel Spector, *The Einsatzgruppen Reports: Selections from the Dispatches of the Nazi Death Squads' Campaign Against the Jews, July 1941–January 1943* (New York: Holocaust Library, 1989), 265.

12   OKW KTB, 1:1085.

13   Quoted in Peter Longerich, *The Unwritten Order: Hitler's Role in the Final Solution* (Charleston, S.C.: Tempus, 2001), 92.

14   Quoted in Peter Klein, ed., *Die Einsatzgruppen in der besetzten Sowjetunion 1941/42: Die Tätigkeits-und Lageberichte des Chefs der Sicherheitspolizei und des SD* (Berlin: Gedenk- und Bildungsstätte Haus der Wannsee-Konferenz, 1997), 280.

15   Quoted in Christopher Browning, *The Origins of the Final Solution: The Evolution of Nazi Jewish Policy, September 1939–March 1942, with contributions by Jürgen Matthäus* (Lincoln: University of Nebraska Press, 2004), 407.

Bibliography

As I said at the start, this book does not represent original scholarship; I have drawn on a great many other historians' works in order to create this introductory survey of Operation *Barbarossa* in both its military and criminal aspects. Unfortunately for most American and English readers, many of the best works are in German, but there are some worthwhile books in English as well. I will touch on some of the most important here.

For a brief insight into the creation of the myths surrounding the Wehrmacht, see the article by James A. Wood, 'Captive Historians, Captivated Audience: The German Military History Program, 1945–1961,' in *The Journal of Military History*, 69/1 (January 2005), 123–47.

There are a great many books on the Nazi state, its relationship to the military, and the lead-up to war. Ian Kershaw's two-volume biography of Hitler is outstanding (*Hitler: 1889–1936: Hubris* and *Hitler: 1936–1945: Nemesis*, both published by W. W. Norton). Omer Bartov's *Mirrors of Destruction* (Oxford: Oxford University Press, 2000) offers a fascinating overview of the cultural and ideological effects of the First World War, as does George Mosse's *Fallen Soldiers: Reshaping the Memory of the World Wars* (New York: Oxford University Press, 1990). Mosse provides further background on Nazi thought in *The Crisis of German Ideology: Intellectual Origins of the Third Reich* (2nd ed.; New York: Schocken Books, 1981). Peter Fritzsche examines German support for Hitler in *Germans into Nazis* (Cambridge: Cambridge University Press, 1998). Vejas Gabriel Liulevicius analyzes German attitudes toward the east in *War Land on the Eastern Front: Culture, National Identity, and German Occupation in World War I* (Cambridge: Cambridge University Press, 2000). Richard Bessel's new work, *Nazism and War* (New York: Modern Library, 2004), is also well worth examining.

Regrettably, some of the best works on German military policy and civil-military relations before the war are not available in English, but *Germany and the Second World War*, by the scholars of the Research Institute for Military History in Potsdam, Germany, contains some excellent essays on the subject; see volume 1, *The Build-up of German Aggression* (Oxford: Clarendon, 1990). Robert J. O'Neill's *The German Army and the Nazi Party, 1933–1939* (London: Cassell, 1966) is also worth reading. Walter Goerlitz, *The German General Staff, 1657–1945* (New York: Praeger, 1953), has long been considered a standard work, but its author was himself a General Staff officer, and it contains a great deal of misleading material.

On the military plans and operations, the best source by far is volume 4, *The Attack on the Soviet Union* (1996), of *Germany and the Second World War*; I would especially recommend the sections by Jürgen Förster on the decision to attack the Soviet Union, by Ernst Klink on the military operations, and by Rolf-Dieter Müller on economic policies and logistics. Volume 1 also provides valuable background material. The text is dense, and the volumes' expense puts them beyond the reach of most readers, but they are invaluable reference tools, and I derived much of the detail in my operational descriptions from them. *Moscow to Stalingrad: Decision in the East* by Earl F. Ziemke and Magna Bauer (New York: Military Heritage Press, 1988) and Albert Seaton, *The Russo-German War, 1941–45* (2nd ed.; Novato, Calif.: Presidio, 1990), are more readable, but neither offers the detail that the Potsdam work does. For the Soviet side, see David Glantz, *Barbarossa: Hitler's Invasion of Russia, 1941* (Stroud, Gloucestershire, UK: Tempus, 2001), as well as John Erickson's *The Road to Stalingrad: Stalin's War with Germany* (2nd ed.; Boulder, Colo.: Westview, 1984). Glantz's examination of Soviet military operations makes his work an excellent companion volume to this one; Erickson goes into more detail but is less readable. *The Halder War Diary, 1939–1942* (edited by Charles Burdick and Hans-Adolf Jacobsen; Novato, Calif.: Presidio, 1988) is among the few published primary sources in English; it is useful, despite its significant abridgments of the original. Beware of the German memoir literature! Books by the likes of Guderian and von Manstein are still selling briskly in English and German, but much of what they contain is not to be trusted, and the same is true for secondary works that depend upon them.

The literature on the crimes is more diverse; that is, one cannot go to just one or two works for a complete picture. For the background developments in Poland I relied heavily on Alexander Rossino's excellent work, *Hitler Strikes Poland: Blitzkrieg, Ideology, and Atrocity* (Lawrence: University Press of Kansas, 2003). For events in the Soviet Union, volume 4 of *Germany and the Second World War* again offers important contributions, especially in Jürgen Förster's sections. Alexander Dallin, *German Rule in Russia, 1941–1945* (2nd ed.; London: Macmillan, 1981), is somewhat out of date but still useful. On the army's role in particular, see Theo Schulte, *The German Army and Nazi Policies in Occupied Russia* (Oxford: Berg, 1989). Christopher Browning and Jürgen Matthäus provide an excellent overview of the crimes against the Jews in *The Origins of the Final Solution: The Evolution of Nazi Jewish Policy, September 1939–March 1942* (Lincoln: University of Nebraska Press, 2004). One should also not fail to consult Raul Hilberg, *The Destruction of the European Jews*, now in its third edition (New Haven, Conn.: Yale University Press, 2003). A new work by Edward B. Westermann, *Hitler's Police Battalions: Enforcing Racial War in the East* (Lawrence: University Press of Kansas, 2005), is an important addition to the literature, as is Ben Shepherd's *War in the Wild East: The German Army and Soviet Partisans* (Cambridge, Mass.: Harvard University Press, 2004). Martin Dean's work, *Collaboration in the Holocaust: Crimes of the Local Police in Belorussia and Ukraine, 1941–44* (New York: St. Martin's Press, 2000; published in association with the United States Holocaust Memorial Museum); Richard Breitman's *The Architect of Genocide: Himmler and the Final Solution* (New York: Knopf, 1991); and Peter Longerich, *The Unwritten Order: Hitler's Role in the Final Solution* (Charleston, S.C.: Tempus, 2001), are also well worth reading. There is, unfortunately, no work in English that deals with the experience of Soviet POWs. Readers of German should consult Christian Streit's *Keine Kameraden: Die Wehrmacht und die sowjetischen Kriegsgefangenen 1941–1945* (2nd ed.; Bonn: Dietz, 1997). Ronald Headland analyzes the reports of the SS killing squads in *Messages of Murder: A Study of the Reports of the Einsatzgruppen of the Security Police and the Security Service, 1941–1943* (Cranbury, N.J.: Associated University Presses, 1992).

There are a couple of general histories that can yield some valuable insights into the German-Soviet war. One is Gerhard Weinberg's master work *A World at Arms: A Global History of World War II* (New York: Cambridge University Press, 1994). And for a broad view of events from the standpoint of the German leadership, see my book *Inside Hitler's High Command* (Lawrence: University Press of Kansas, 2000).

Finally, for a broader view of the literature, I recommend Rolf-Dieter Müller and Gerd R. Ueberschär, *Hitler's War in the East: A Critical Assessment* (2nd ed.; New York: Berghahn, 2002), especially parts C, D, and E.

List of Illustrations

MAPS

All maps were created by the author using the Xara X[1] graphics program.

Index

Index

Index

223

TEMPUS – REVEALING HISTORY

Private 12768 Memoir of a Tommy
JOHN JACKSON

'Unique... a beautifully written, strikingly honest account of a young man's experience of combat' **Saul David**

'At last we have John Jackson's intensely personal and heartfelt little book to remind us there was a view of the Great War other than Wilfred Owen's' **The Daily Mail**

£9.99   0 7524 3531 0

The German Offensives of 1918
MARTIN KITCHEN

'A lucid, powerfully driven narrative' **Malcolm Brown**
'Comprehensive and authoritative... first class'
Holger H. Herwig

£13.99   0 7524 3527 2

Verdun 1916
MALCOLM BROWN

'A haunting book which gets closer than any other to that wasteland marked by death'
Richard Holmes

£9.99   0 7524 2599 4

The Forgotten Front
The East African Campaign 1914–1918
ROSS ANDERSON

'Excellent... fills a yawning gap in the historical record'
The Times Literary Supplement
'Compelling and authoritative'
Hew Strachan

£25   0 7524 2344 4

Agincourt
A New History
ANNE CURRY

'A highly distinguished and convincing account'
Christopher Hibbert
'A *tour de force*' **Alison Weir**
'*The* book on the battle' **Richard Holmes**
A **BBC History Magazine** Book of the Year 2005

£25   0 7524 2828 4

The Welsh Wars of Independence
DAVID MOORE

'Beautifully written, subtle and remarkably perceptive' **John Davies**

£25   0 7524 3321 0

Bosworth 1485 Psychology of a Battle
MICHAEL K. JONES

'Most exciting... a remarkable tale' **The Guardian**
'Insightful and rich study of the Battle of Bosworth... no longer need Richard play the villain' **The Times Literary Supplement**

£12.99   0 7524 2594 3

The Battle of Hastings 1066
M.K. LAWSON

'Blows away many fundamental assumptions about the battle of Hastings... an exciting and indispensable read' **David Bates**
A **BBC History Magazine** Book of the Year 2003

£25   0 7524 2689 3